Heaven and Hell
Belief in Life after death for the 21st century.

By

Alexander Wynd

Heaven and Hell.
Belief in Life after death for the 21st century.

Author
Alexander Wynd

ISBN 978-0-9559789-0-6
Printed by Lulu.com
2008

Acknowledgements

Biblical texts are from the New Revised Standard Version of the Bible.

Copyright notice. The Scripture portions contained herein are from the Revised Standard Version of the Bible. Anglicised Edition copyright 1989 1996 the Division of Christian Education of the National Council of the churches of Christ of the United States of America and are used by permission. All rights reserved.

I would like to acknowledge the help of the Rev Andrew Morton, who read the book and made suggestions.

I would like to acknowledge the help of the staff of Cupar library who managed to obtain some rather obscure books.

Grateful thanks are due to my family for their help and patience with me.

Contents
1 Introduction. The purpose and readership of the book.
2 Time and Eternity: Past: Future: Space: Other worlds:
3 The Soul or mind or self. Beliefs about the mind: Dualism: Monism: Christian belief: Descartes.
4 Death. What happens when we die: four possible positions regarding the soul or self: near death experiences: the story of Er: other near death experiences: Spiritualism and the hereafter: where could Heaven and Hell be in relation to our universe: the resurrection of the body: disembodied existence: permanent and temporary disembodied existence: dreams: summary.
5 The Hereafter: The Resurrection appearances of Jesus: three conclusions about the appearances: the traditional doctrine of the hereafter: the goal of our existence.
6 Heaven: Introduction: St. Salvius: Historical: Biblical ideas- Paradise- the Kingdom of God- Rest –Glory –Peace- Life.
The Greek view of the afterlife: Old Testament passages: New Testament passages: Church fathers and summary of their ideas: Mediaeval ideas -Contemplative –mystical-popular –poetical (Dante): Reformers: Victorian: Twentieth century: Heaven on earth: Ways to describe heaven now: Beatific vision: heaven as seeing and being with family and friends: heaven as home: heaven as a beautiful place: beauty: Joy and heaven: Happiness and heaven: Our conscience and heaven.
What is Heaven like and do we have any possible glimmerings of it in this life: Music: Scent: Art: Architecture: Photography: Films: Comic Strips: Videos: Poetry and literature: Tales of ghosts: Thin places: People: Saints:
Life in Heaven: What will happen to us in heaven: static heaven: eternal rest: peace: dynamic heaven.
What will our bodies be like: our post resurrection bodies: do we go immediately to heaven after death: intermediate stage: Biblical: conclusions.
Concluding comment on the chapter on heaven
7 Purgatory
8 Hell-
Introduction- Hell in Plato. Biblical Words: Old Testament word: Sheol: New Testament words Gehenna, Hades: Tartarus: Summary of Biblical words used.
Summary of hell in Gospels: Paul's epistles and Hell: James, 2 Peter and Revelation and hell: Summary of descriptions of hell in New Testament: warnings: rejection: retribution: Resurrection of the wicked: Church fathers and hell: Mediaeval view of hell: Reformers

and hell: Victorians and hell: Twentieth century and hell.
What is hell like: Ways to describe Hell now -the Brochure.
What is hell like: gloom: lack of beauty: discord: hate:
meaninglessness: loss and separation from God.
Indicators of hell in art: photography: films.
Seven views about Hell-
1 Extinction or annihilation.
2 Destruction
3 Everlasting punishment. Is hell eternal?
4 Everlasting torture
5 Punishment with a future in heaven.
6 A vague existence forever.
7 Purification.
Universalism or Universal salvation or conditional salvation:
Arguments for universal salvation: The New Testament passages
The church fathers: modern arguments about universal salvation:
Arguments against universal salvation: summary for and against.
Selected for hell. Are you abandoned in hell? Who is going to hell?
Predestination, election and Freewill: historical summary.
Some other things about hell: Where is Hell in relation to our world:
Prayer for the dead: What abut those who never heard the gospel?
The devil and Hell: Summary of the doctrine of hell.
9 The Communion of Saints -Savonarola.
10 The Judgement of the dead
Ancient times: Biblical: Old Testament views on judgement: New
Testament and judgement: Biblical names of Judgement: Church
fathers: Creeds and Judgement: Mediaeval: Aquinas: Dante:
The two great judgements. Judgement of the nations: Individual
judgement or the particular judgement.
Who is judge of us all? Who will be judged? Does what we did
matter when we are being judged? When will we be judged? How
can I be sure that whatever judgement is given that it will be just?
What about mercy? Can we condemn other people?
The Good News: The Great Assize: The morality of Judgement:
Jesus as Saviour and as Judge: Self knowledge: Last judgement
and Art:
Summarising the Last Judgement.
11 The Second Coming.
Biblical views- Old Testament: New Testament: Timing of the event:
Early Church and the timing: modern views: end of the world or
universe: Is the kingdom of heaven here now: what is to happen:
art: hymns: Millenarianism: The theology of hope: Problems of the
Second Coming. Summary.

12 Conclusions.
13 Appendices.
Texts on heaven, hell and judgement.
List of some pictures on Heaven Hell and Judgement.
List of films
Book list.

Chapter 1

Introduction
The purpose and readership of the book.

Christians of previous generations had the privilege of listening to many sermons on heaven, hell and judgement. These sermons have all but completely vanished from our churches. When did you, reader, last hear a sermon on any of these subjects? The sermons on this subject belong to the past, but the need to know about our future destiny is still there. Death is inevitable for all of us. What do we say to those who have lost a loved one?

This book is aimed at Christians and also people of other faiths, who wish to know about life after death. Most theological books on the subject of life after death cannot be understood by most of us. Why are these theological books incomprehensible? These books are really like computer manuals. If you are a computer boffin, you really want all the detail of what a computer does, but the rest of us do not need to know every detail. Similarly the theologian uses words and phrases which are very difficult to most of us. Some theologians quote large chunks of foreign languages. One book, which is in the book list, has lines and lines of Latin, Greek, Hebrew, French and German. No doubt this was because the author was familiar with these languages and was trying to reproduce exact quotations, but this practice is very infuriating to anyone unfamiliar with all these languages. Also even the English words in some theological books are quite difficult. A few examples of words, which are found in theological books, are "ontic", "metempsychosis", "pelagianism", "soteriological" "apocatastasis" and "perichoresis". It becomes a really difficult task to read a book with words like these.

This book is comprehensive and various difficult questions are raised. Instead of just using words, references to films, pictures, photography and videos are included in order to give a comprehensive idea of what the future of people after death might be. Readers need to develop their own ideas and not be afraid to think that the author has "got it wrong".

One final word in the introduction. The hereafter is the one subject, which has not given rise to controversy or indeed the cry of heresy. We shall not really know about the life after death, until it happens to us. Until then we must have faith that we shall live again in heaven.

The Bible
The books of the Bible will be familiar to most of the readers of this book. The Apocrypha is a number of books, which were not part of the Hebrew Bible, but which the early Church accepted as being inspired by God. Some of these books especially Sirach, Wisdom, Judith and 1 and 2 Maccabees are quoted
In this book. The Roman Catholic Church accepted these books, so they are found in the Jerusalem Bible. The reformers did not accept them, so they are only found as an addition in other Bibles, so if you wish to read them you need an edition with the Apocrypha. Some other old Jewish books are also quoted.

Chapter 2

TIME and ETERNITY

Time and eternity present a puzzle to us. We are paid by time. So much per hour or day or week is a common way of being paid. We look to the clock for our appointments. We remember events, which happened in the near or distant past. Time is very important to us. Yet there are other ways of thinking. The seasons are not measured in hours, minutes and seconds. Harvest time can range from the end of July until October, although cereals have been harvested in January in Fife. Two cereal harvests in one year have happened in one particularly wet season. A child thinks that time passes slowly at school, but speeds up when playing games after school. The dying seconds of a football game when you are winning 3-2 passes very slowly.

Theologians recognise three kinds of time.

Firstly, there is continuous or solar time (also sidereal time). This is the time by which we measure our lives and also history.

Secondly, there is discontinuous or spiritual time. A thought can be for an instant in spiritual time, but this can last for two hours in solar time.

Thirdly, there is eternity or God's life. In God there is no past nor future, but only an eternal present. We will participate in eternity after we come to heaven, which is after death. There is nothing beyond eternity and we will be there forever.

PAST

There are other problems with time. People have recounted seeing the ghostly battle of Edgehill being fought, although it was fought some 350 years ago. Instances occur of persons seeing ghostly highwaymen or of Roman soldiers marching along a road some feet below the present day ground. One story about the past in the present is of Archbishop Sharp's coach, which has been seen flying on towards St. Andrew's centuries after his murder.
Are these ghostly events real? They would appear to be so to the persons, who have experienced them. If it is not imagination, then we must postulate that sometimes we see things that are out of our normal time sequence. This is not a daily occurrence, but happens to only some people and just occasionally, perhaps once in their lifetime. There must be other sequences of time other than chronological time. Perhaps the past can sometimes be seen now,

but cannot be affected by us.

FUTURE

Can we see the future? It is common in the Highlands of Scotland for some persons to have the Second Sight, which is seeing the future. This is often a foreboding of death, where the person sees a coffin of a relative or friend who is still alive to his knowledge but who is about to die. It also frequently happens when someone is dying a distance away, yet the person can see or feel that it is happening now. Strangely it is quite common among certain peoples, particularly the Celtic tribes and their modern day descendants, the Irish, the Gaelic Scots and the Welsh. Unfortunately, this ability is often lost or becomes latent in the modern world.

There are also seers. These men can see into the future. One of the most notable was the Brahan seer of Rosshire. He made many forecasts, some of which came true several centuries later. Examples of these were that he forecasted aeroplanes and the Caledonian Canal. He could also see present day happenings at a distance. This was his undoing. The Countess of Seaforth asked him if he could see what her husband was doing at the present time. The seer was unwilling to reply, but she compelled him to tell the truth. The seer replied that he could see the Earl of Seaforth in a room with a lady. The Countess was furious and had the Brahan seer burned in a barrel. The seer then forecast the inglorious end of the Seaforth family, which came true.

In Corsica there are mazzeru who have mysterious powers, who go out in the middle of the night and see scenes, which only they can see e.g. the funeral of a villager who is not yet dead.
So there is no sequence of past, present, future as is assumed in modern thought. Past, present and future can all exist at the same time and events of all three ages can be seen and can happen to at least some people. Perhaps we all have this ability, but it has become lost to us.

SPACE

Are heaven and hell in space and how do these states relate to our present world? We talk about heaven being up there, but this does not necessarily imply that heaven is up in the sky. The poet Dante located hell in the centre of the earth, but then he had to locate it somewhere. Heaven and hell are not physical places, as

we think of physical places e.g. Edinburgh. Heaven and hell are not even located somewhere out in space. They belong to a different existence, sometimes called the spiritual world. This existence must have some relationship to the present world and could be another dimension (for want of a better word) of our present universe.
We know that the things on this Universe including ourselves are not little bits of solid matter, but are something like electrical impulses and space at the sub-atomic level at least. So this leaves room for other worlds, other universes co-existing with our universe or other spheres of existence in the present universe. What these other spaces are like we do not know, but it makes the location of heaven and hell much less fanciful. And it provides some sort of explanation for the very mysterious events on our present earth. One kind of mysterious event that it is difficult to explain within our present knowledge is the external manifestations of the mystics. One example is the mysticism of St. Teresa of Avila. She floated above the church floor and had to grasp the Communion rail in order to avoid floating to the roof, when she took Communion. There are other similar bizarre events, which have a religious foundation such as bilocation, which is being in two different places at the same time. These events have no physical basis. They belong to somewhere beyond this Universe or at least a different and much more complex universe from what we usually perceive.

OTHER WORLDS

It would be wrong not to mention other worlds, so familiar to us in space fiction. The Universe is far, far bigger than we ever visualised or can visualise, if we believe the statisticians. There is no good reason to suppose that they can make predictions from one single event (the existence of our solar system), if indeed it is unique. But we must also recognise that in a very extensive universe, there possibly may be other worlds in which human life could exist. If this is so, then we must say something to account for this in relation to our theology. God is God of the whole universe, no matter how big it could be. But God's concern is for us and He surely must have that concern for other thinking beings, if indeed they do exist.

If these other beings exist do they have or do they need another Saviour? Is Jesus the only Saviour of the whole universe? If little green or purple humanoids exist out there and they are not sinless, do they have a Saviour of their own? We cannot say yes or no. For that question to be answered, we would need to wait until they discover us or we discover them. But it is likely that they would have to go to heaven too when they die, if they are thinking beings like us.

Finally, the other worlds would not be heaven. Some theologians have thought that heaven could be on a far distant planet like earth. And we would go there when we die and be embodied again. But a more reasonable explanation is that another planet would be like earth, needing God's intervention and a having a distant heaven and maybe even hell too.

Chapter 3

The SOUL or MIND or SELF

"The souls of the righteous are in the hand of God and there shall no torment touch them." [1]

BELIEFS ABOUT THE MIND

The idea of the soul or mind or self has caused discussion throughout the ages, but has been generally accepted until the present. There have been two extreme views as to what human beings are, as well as varying intermediate positions. The idea of the soul is not just a major belief for Christians and the theistic religions, but atheists too must consider the idea, which is fundamental for all humanity. Without some idea of the self or soul or mind, then we are just a group of sense impressions co-ordinated by the brain. If that is true, then there is no hereafter for us.

There are two main beliefs about the soul or mind with many variations in between. These beliefs are dualism and monism. Christian belief about the soul is somewhere in between these two beliefs.

DUALISM

At one extreme end of the spectrum of belief, philosophers have described the relation between mind and body as dualistic. This means that there are two separate entities, body and soul (or mind). The idea of a separate body and soul goes back to Plato, one of the major Greek philosophers.

Plato, like his master Socrates, had ethical motives and struggled to work out arguments for the immortality of the soul. Plato regarded the soul, as the principle of life and for that very reason was immortal. The soul had an essential affinity with the eternal spiritual ideas of the good, true and beautiful. The soul was not visible, composite, or material like the body, which was its prison, but the soul was simple, spiritual and divine and thus could not be dissolved. Nor can the soul have acquired this knowledge of the great spiritual ideas from existing material reality. This knowledge of the great spiritual ideas can be derived only from

---

[1] Wisdom 3:1

memory, from the time of a previous life that the soul must have led before it entered into this matter, into this concrete body. By death, this free spirit soul is released again from the body, its prison and tomb. It is purified by rebirths and can eventually be again united with the divine. The spirit soul is immortal and this very fact should determine the individual and social life of mortal human beings here and now.

This idea of a completely separate body and soul is not part of Christian belief but many Christian thinkers have gone part of the way to endorsing this idea. But the idea is part of Hindu belief, where the separate soul enters another body after death. This is called reincarnation. The soul could enter another human body, but could also enter an animal body. This entry and re-entry into a body could go on many times in a never-ending circle, only broken by the end of the universe.

Plato's thought was disputed. Aristotle claimed immortality only for the supra individual world soul. Augustine followed Plato. Averros and the Mediaeval Arab philosophers followed Aristotle. Albert the Great and Aquinas as well as Descartes, Leibnitz and Wolff followed Plato and attempted to substantiate philosophically the immortality of the soul.

MONISM

The opposing position to dualism is monism i.e. body and soul are one. People who believe in this are called epiphenomenalists. They believe that the mind or soul cannot exist separately from the body although some Monists would say that the mind is real. Most Monists do not believe that thinking is solely a natural process, involving the brain only. Atheists, who are extreme Monists, disbelieve that a mind or soul exists at all and the only true person is the body alone.

CHRISTIAN BELIEF

The middle position between dualism and monism has been held by Christians as well as by others. Christians (and other theistic religions) do not believe that the soul is completely independent of and unaffected by the body. They also do not believe that the soul is naturally immortal. Christians do not believe that the soul could pre-exist the body. They also do not believe that the soul, existing before the person is born, could just enter anybody the soul so chose at birth. Theistic belief is that the soul

comes into being when a person is born and develops as the body develops from birth. On the other hand Christians believe that the soul does not depend on the earthly body for existence, but survives the death of the body, and takes on a new body in heaven. This new body is sometimes called the spiritual body.
The soul is the principle of life in traditional Christian thought. Human beings are rational souls in that they think and choose freely. The soul is what makes a human being distinct from an animal body and the body and soul are one substance. This is called a psychophysical entity. Christians believe that the components of human beings i.e. the body and the soul can be distinguished. This is different from the monist view that soul and body cannot be distinguished, so that the soul or person does not survive bodily death.

Descartes

One philosopher who asked questions regarding his own identity was Descartes. His famous saying was "I think, therefore I am" Descartes wanted a foundation to build a philosophical system and this system started from his own thoughts. The reason for this was that he could reject everything else.

Descartes rejected sense impressions as a foundation because he said the senses sometimes "play us false." He also rejected knowledge based on human reasoning because he noted that humans made mistakes in reasoning. He found that you could doubt everything except that the doubter could not doubt the reality of his own doubting. Because only an existent being could doubt, the doubter must exist and that thinking must be part of his identity. Although Descartes' ideas have been criticised, the system comprising soul or mind or self existing apart from the body, although closely identified with it, has been a part of Christian thought for centuries.

Chapter 4

DEATH

What happens when we die?

The answers given by Christians and the followers of other religions until recent times are that we go to another existence, which is dwelling in heaven or hell. That this is not only a Christian belief can be seen in early Egypt, where the dead were buried with material possessions in order to help them in the afterlife. Also, in Greece, as early as the time of Homer (about 900 BC) the dead were thought to have souls, which, after death, were in Hades. There are problems about the soul surviving the body. It is indeed the idea of survival without a body has been difficult to understand. How can we call ourselves living when our mortal body is 'mouldering' in the grave or has been burned by cremation until only the ashes remain? And where indeed are heaven and hell and how do they relate to our cosmology?

The ancients never believed that heaven was a physical place somewhere in the sky or hell was somewhere in the ground. The three dimensional world, so criticised by Bultmann and his successor theologians was not a true reality. The other worlds were spiritual, which could be anywhere. True, this three dimensional world is found in the cosmology of the poet Dante, who constructed in his poems a gigantic theoretical cosmology. In his poems, there was an entrance to hell on this earth where Dante accompanied by the poet Virgil descended. The two persons travelled deeper and deeper into hell, meeting various dead persons who were placed according to the gravity of their sins. Sceptics make that picture concrete, in order to pour scorn on the idea of heaven and hell. The materialism, that is a product of nineteenth century physics, is also partly responsible for the lack of belief in heaven and hell. Dalton's atomic theory of 1806, conceived the world as composed of small material particles called atoms. It is exceedingly difficult to fit another–worldly dimension into this very materialistic picture of the world.

There is, among philosophers, a fiercely fought battle concerning the existence of the soul. The soul or self or mind was seen to be inseparable from the body and that there was nothing apart from the physical body. On this view, at death, the body dissolves and the person is no more.

When the body dies, does the soul or self cease to exist? Until recent times this has not been considered at all. We cannot conceive a disembodied person, but we might conceive a resurrected person with a new body.

Four possible positions regarding the soul or self.

To summarise, there are four possible positions regarding the soul or mind or self with regard to the hereafter.

1) No soul or mind or self exists, but only the physical body. This means that there is no life after death. This is the atheist position. Only material things exist. There is no mind or soul or self, only a body and a brain, which receives sense impressions and acts upon them. Feuerbach, who lived 150 years ago, gave an explanation for the theist view that there is life after death. He described a future life as wishful thinking and most atheists since have followed his ideas. The answer to the atheists is the direct opposite i.e. the belief that this life is all that there exists is also wishful thinking. This belief of there not being any hereafter means that there is no judgement and no reckoning of how you have lived your life and no possibility of hell. This idea could also be very much described as wishful thinking. The position of the atheists on this subject seems much more likely to be wishful thinking than the alternative idea of a future life.

2) The soul is pre-existent and so it is naturally immortal. This is the extreme dualist position. The soul or self or mind is a ghost in a machine. The soul could be reincarnated in another person or could exist independently of the body.

3) Another way that we could be resurrected is if the soul is in union with God and Jesus and has no independent existence, but is completely absorbed in God. We would then live in a mystical union with Him. The mystics longed for this in their present lives without success, even though they had mystical experiences. But they also believed that the mystical union would come after death. The idea of the union with the Divine is not confined to Christian mystics but is believed by other mystics too. Summarising mysticism, could some Christians have mystical union with the divine God? And not just Christians can have these experiences. Muslims too can have mystical experiences: a good example was Al Hallaj, who was put to death because of his mysticism.

4) The soul exists in the future after death because of the death and resurrection of Jesus and is an embodied soul or self. Christians, who believe in Jesus and His resurrection, believe in a resurrected body. This has Biblical confirmation, as St. Paul compared our

resurrection body like a seed and a plant. This analogy has been severely criticised, but it should be remembered that this is only an analogy and analogies are never perfect. If you could describe something clearly, there would not be any need for an analogy. Paul's point was surely that the resurrection body would have something in common with our own body but would be totally unlike in appearance. If we believe in a resurrection body there would need to be something in common with the body before resurrection and this could be the essential self or the soul or mind. But it would not have the same particles as before i.e. not the same protons or electrons or the same sub atomic particles, but would be made up of a different kind of substance. This would be needed if we were to be recognisable as persons and could do things other than pure thought. In short, while we cannot say what the other substance could be, we believe that the soul exists. The idea that, when we dwell in heaven, we would only be able to achieve pure thought might be wonderful to some academics or contemplatives, but could never satisfy the rest of us.

Near death experiences. The story of Er, son of Armenius a native of Pamphylia.

Er was killed in battle, and when the dead were taken up on the tenth day and the rest of the dead soldiers were already decomposing, Er was still quite sound. He was taken home and he was to be buried on the twelfth day after he died. Er was already lying on the funeral pyre, when he came to life again and told the story of what he had seen in the other world. He said that when his soul left his body it travelled in company with many others till they up came to a wonderfully strange place. In that place there were, close to each other, two gaping chasms in the earth, and opposite and above them two other chasms in the sky. Between the chasms sat judges, who, having delivered a judgement, ordered the just to take the right hand road that led up through the sky, and fastened the badge of their judgement in front of them. At the same time, they ordered the unjust, who carried the badges of all they had done behind them, to take the left-hand road that led them downwards. When Er came before them, they said that he was to be a messenger to men about the other world, and ordered him to listen to and watch all that went on in that place. He then saw the souls, when judgement had been passed on them, departing, some by one of the heavenly chasms and some by one of the earthly chasms. At the same time, by the other two chasms some souls rose out of the earth, stained with the dust of travel, and others descended from heaven, pure and clean. And the throng of souls surviving seem to have come from long journey, and turned aside gladly into the meadow and encamped there as for a festival; acquaintances exchanged greetings, and those from earth and those from heaven enquired each others experiences. And those from earth told theirs with sorrow and tears as they told all they had suffered and seen on the journey, which lasted for a thousand years. But the others told of the delights of heaven and of the wonderful beauty of what they had seen. [2]

Other near death experiences

One of the interesting "proofs" of the person or soul or self or mind and also of a future life is the large number of reported near death experiences. These near death experiences can vary but a typical case is described in the following paragraph. The person near to death can then hear a doctor pronouncing death. There is a sense of floating and looking down on one's own body. Often the person reporting these events can recall the whole area below him or her. Sometimes they can see things, which are not visible from their bodily position e.g. seeing objects lying on top of cupboards in the room. The person has a feeling of going along a long dark tunnel. The person is then at a distance from their body and can see the people around them.

Eventually, the person discovers a different body with new properties and powers. Other people come and help as well as relatives who have died previously. A warm loving spirit is encountered and gives a playback of a former life. However a barrier is encountered and a voice says to go back, that your time is not yet come. There is a great feeling of reluctance to go back, but that is what happens.

These events are hard to explain on the phenomenalist theory that the mind is identical to the brain. Do these instances prove the existence of the separateness of the soul or is there an explanation which will yet be found and which is not yet apparent? Any explanations have just not so far accounted for all the facts.
One rationalistic explanation is that near to death the brain changes its chemical nature and sees things differently or has a different interpretation on what it sees than what it normally would. Whether this is a full explanation for these events is doubtful. The alternative

---

[2] Plato's Republic book 10

is that humans are sometimes given a foretaste of their immediate future after death.

These experiences are interesting and also may give some idea of what happens after death. But it must be remembered that these experiences take place when the person is not yet dead. These experiences are perhaps a foretaste of heaven, but are not descriptions of heaven. The recipients of these experiences are still here on earth, when they experience these things.
Another point is that similar things happen when persons are in other states e.g. under the influence of drugs or in mystical states. It is really difficult to determine what these things mean. Of course, it is possible that they may be experiencing some kind of knowledge of the future after death.

Spiritualism and the hereafter

Most of the churches except the Christian Spiritualist churches are rather wary of spiritualism or any attempt to contact dead people. The main biblical text about raising the dead is found in first Samuel and is about the Woman of Endor, who, at the command of Saul, raised the dead Samuel. Samuel said, "Why have you disturbed me, bringing me up." [3] Samuel warned Saul of his imminent fate. This fate was to be Saul's own death and of the death of his family in a battle with the Philistines. This story has been taken by Christians as a warning not to attempt to learn of their future fate by raising up the dead.

Spiritualism has sometimes been popular. This happened particularly after the First World War when there were so many bereaved widows. These widows wanted to know something about the fate of the dead husbands. But today is a sceptical and indifferent age and belief in spiritualism has waned.
The claims of spiritualism to be able to contact people on the other side are not completely convincing. It is not too clear where the mediums have obtained their information about these dead people. This information may come from the deceased or it could come from living people by telepathy, or there could be many explanations.

If you wish to learn more about spiritualism, there is a book "Adventures in immortality" by a Church of Scotland minister D A Kennedy. Atheists of course, deny the existence of contact with the dead, deny the existence of telepathy, just as they deny the

---

[3] 1 Samuel 28:7 etc.

existence of hypnotism. (Atheists at one time denied that meteorites existed.) They put spiritualism down to straight fraud or delusion, but this is unfair. There could be other explanations for spiritualism as well as having contact with the dead.

The main conclusion about spiritualism is that the evidence of contact with the dead is unproven. Even if their evidence is accepted, it is still not evidence for heaven, as envisaged by Christians.

Where could Heaven and Hell be in relation to our Universe?

It is conceived by our present day science that our worlds and indeed our selves are non-material (at least at the sub-atomic level). The body is not made up of individual atoms but instead is a large amount of space along with a number of tiny particles, which may just be electrical impulses. This is the universe conceived by present day physics and not the very material science of the nineteenth century. This could mean that there is another dimension where we ourselves could live after we have passed on from this life. In fact there could be many such dimensions. Jesus gives testimony to the belief that there are many other dimensions and this will be explored more fully in the next chapter. If we are to take the New Testament seriously, the appearances of Jesus were not like anything we have known either now or since Jesus was alive. He was unique. But He gives testimony to a life beyond death.

The ideas of heaven, hell, the last judgement and the Communion of Saints have been a traditional part of the Church's teaching throughout the centuries. Fortunately there has not been very much controversy about these ideas within Christians of various denominations (however unpalatable these might be to atheists or humanists) as compared with other Christian teachings, particularly about the nature of the Church. It has been accepted that we can have very differing views about these subjects, without being heretical.

However in this modern age, the idea of an afterlife has not been unchallenged. The idea of a material world has permeated our thinking. If all existence is composed of solid atoms, it does not leave much space in the universe for an afterlife. In the Middle Ages, Dante conceived of hell as somewhere in the middle of the Earth. That possibility is closed to us and we must conceive heaven and hell as places outwith our normal space-time continuum. The suggestions that we are revived on another planet in the solar system are somewhat ridiculous.

The Resurrection of the body

One of the articles in the Apostles Creed is the resurrection of the Body. This belief seems impossible to us today, as we know that what we call our body is after death mouldering in the grave, in the depths of the ocean, or a pile of burnt ashes scattered on the hillside. We do not really see our individual atoms being brought together and reconstituted as we were in life. There are also difficulties with that idea. We know that our bodies are constantly changing and our body is certainly not the same as it was when we are babies. Also the body deteriorates as we go into old age. Augustine said we would not be resurrected as an old man or woman, but as a young person of thirty. We probably do not want our bodies to be reconstituted as they were at the moment of death, especially if we died of a very painful illness.

What does this phrase resurrection of the body really mean, if we are not reconstituted exactly as we were? We must do away with very materialistic views of our body and cannot think of our bodies as somehow reconstituted as they were. This would mean that individual atoms or other particles would somehow be collected by miraculous means after death and then be rebuilt as the original body, as some of the Church Fathers thought.

We take up the idea of an embodied soul or self. We do not believe that the soul pre-exists the body, then enters it at birth and thus leaves the body at death. We cannot, like the Greeks, talk of the soul entombed in the body and which effects a release from the body at death. The soul or self is a whole with the body and unless the whole dies, we must describe the soul after death as having a resurrected body. And the thought of another existence in another dimension (which we call heaven) seems feasible; it would seem logical for our soul to be dwelling there with a new body. This does not necessarily mean a material body, as we understand a material body, but at least a body which can be seen and which can interact with other people.

Summary of the resurrection of the body ideas.

The phrase "Resurrection of the body" has important truths that we must not forget.

Firstly, the belief that all of us will not be incorporated into God. The mystics wish closer union with God, but we must not be so close to God, that we lose our individual identity. We will be recognisable, as persons to those who have known us here on earth. We will have all the recognisable elements e.g. our face, our hands and the other parts of our bodies. Besides having an identity the idea of a bodily existence means that there will be real continuity between our life here on earth and our body in heaven. If this is so, it means that what we do here in this world, ultimately matters in eternity. What we are and what we do is ultimately taken up into heaven when we die. There cannot be a physical continuity between this life and the next, as the atoms, which constitute our body now, will not be the same matter which makes up our bodies in heaven. We must also take into account that the physical atoms, which make up our existence, are not really physical, but would appear to be constituted of something else, possibly energy. When we talk of a resurrected body there must be some kind of material reality.

Secondly, the idea of a bodily resurrection means that our existence in heaven is real and not imaginary. Some people see ghosts at some time in their lives. But these ghosts may not be real people now, but some kind of vision or picture or trace of these people as they were in the past. The ghostly rider on horseback is a real rider out of time and we might think of time as being the unreal factor. But our life in heaven is not an insubstantial trace of us as we are on Earth. We are in heaven as a real existence, and a completely different life. The hymn says "fuller sweeter is the life and ample ampler is the air". Heaven is not like our life here, but is a far, far better life than we had on earth.

Thirdly, the idea of a purely spiritual future existence is excluded. It is often thought that we have both a body and a soul and these have separate identities. The soul is conceived as existing within the body, and is released form the body at death. Often quoted at funerals, the words of the Wisdom of Solomon are "the souls of the righteous are in the hands of God and there shall no torment touch them." We commit his or her body to the earth as if his or her soul is elsewhere. If we talk of the resurrection of the body, we dismiss the idea of the soul remaining separate from any kind of body in a future existence.

Disembodied existence.

In order to be recognisable, we need another body. If we do not have another body we will not be able to communicate with one another or even see each other. This can be permanent or temporary.

Permanent disembodied existence
One form of disembodied existence is the soul surviving as pure mind. This existence may not just be pure thought, but we could visualise a form of telepathic communication between souls and even memory of a life on earth. However possible in theory, this has never had a place in Christian thought.
Temporary disembodied existence.
However there is also the question of whether the soul can exist temporarily on its own. This is the common belief among Christians, that after our own bodily death, the soul survives, awaiting the general resurrection. This could be described as an intermediate state in that the soul exists, but needs the body for a full existence, and this happens at Resurrection Day. At that time the body becomes re-united with the soul.

This can happen in two ways: either the old physical body is collected piece by piece or atom by atom and is by a miraculous act of God, then re-united with the body. The other way is that the soul will be transformed into a glorified body or spiritual body. Paul describes this glorified body as being similar to the relationship between a seed and a plant. The seed looks completely different to a plant, but becomes a plant. So in a similar way our resurrection body is similar to our present living body but is completely different. However, we must not press the seed plant analogy too far.
The new spiritual body would have several different properties (according to Irenaeus, Augustine and Aquinas): i.e.
Perfection
Immune to evil
Will not suffer
Needs neither food nor drink

The intermediate period gives some difficulties and seems to be due to confusion between time - our earthly time and the eternal. A thousand ages in Thy sight are like a morning gone," says the hymn. So Jesus said to the condemned thief who was crucified along with Him "Today you will be with me in Paradise". We need not think of an intermediate period because there is no time in eternity. Whether it is a millionth of a second or 900 million years in earth time before the End, the time interval is the same in the hereafter. (The 900 million years is the time calculated for the Sun to come too close to the Earth.)

Cullman, a famous theologian would not agree with me here. He said dead persons are in time. But how can dead persons be in time? Time belongs to we who are living on Earth. If the idea of an intermediate period is abandoned, this does away with two difficulties. These difficulties are the prospect of a disembodied soul existing temporarily on its own and the clear message in the Bible that we will have immediate entry to heaven.

Dreams

Some idea of the "other" can be thought from the world of our dreams. Many dreams have physical causes. Sometimes there are reasons or fears in our everyday existence, which can lead to dreams. But, just occasionally in our waking world, there are dreams which are different and which could give an indication of the future or at least indicate that this world is not just about money, politics and football. Some writers have even indicated that the future world would be like a dream world, but that is supposing too much.

The Bible however places some importance on certain dreams. Sometimes these dreams have a religious content and some indicate events, which, after interpretation, will actually take place. Joseph was able to interpret the dreams of Pharaoh's baker and butler with devastating consequences for one of them (Pharaoh hanged the chief baker). Nebuchadnezzar had a very devastating dream in the book of Daniel and Sarah and Ahimelech also had dreams.

The significance of dreams is that they sometimes indicate the consequences for an individual and sometimes the future of a nation, just as Joseph's dream of the seven fat years and the seven lean years was of great importance for the Egyptians. Dreams remind us that the physical world is not all there is.

Summary

The identity of the soul or self or mind is the main theme of this chapter. The crucial question for Christianity and indeed for all theism is the rejection of the self as being identical with the body including the brain. Instead the traditional doctrine of the soul or self which is in close conjunction with the body but is not identical to it is essential for Christianity. This doctrinal position can also take into account near death experiences and ISP (Sensory Perception) researches. If we adopt a dualist position, i.e. that we comprise both body and soul, even if not an extreme dualist position, we can more easily justify a belief in the hereafter, where the soul (which is really me) can dwell. The fact that we do not really know about life after death, but can only guess, does not really matter too much.

With so much in life, we make judgements without real personal evidence. The idea of a hereafter depends on the way we perceive God and the life of Jesus. If we feel that there is more to life than what we experience and that our knowledge of Jesus is such that there is more to life than this existence, then we at least have some evidence for what we believe will happen to us in the hereafter.

Chapter 5

THE HEREAFTER

The resurrection appearances of Jesus, the traditional doctrine of the hereafter and the goal of our existence.

The Resurrection appearances of Jesus

The basis of the Christian belief in the hereafter is the crucifixion of Jesus, the empty tomb and the resurrection appearances of Jesus. The theology of the Crucifixion and does not concern us here (it is called Soteriology). And the empty tomb is not a critical issue for the belief in the resurrection. The texts on the empty tomb will not be considered here. These texts are important, but they do not add anything to what we believe will happen in the life to come. The Resurrection appearances of Jesus have been the subject of considerable criticism, particularly in recent years. If you want to read a criticism Peter Carnley's book "The structure of resurrection belief" gives an unfair criticism of the reality of these appearances, which he states are purely subjective. Carnley also stated that you couldn't take the appearances recorded in First Corinthians, and Luke's gospel and John's gospel and make a coherent account of these appearances. Most New Testament scholars would accept Carnley's view. However, these scholars find it difficult to accept a Jesus, who can be seen, was mostly insubstantial and who sometimes appeared to be more solid than on other occasions, so that sometimes He could even eat.

What are these appearances? They are stated in three Gospels only, as the ending of Mark's gospel has been lost. They are also found in Paul's first letter to the Corinthians chapter 15. The appearance of Jesus to Paul (on the road to Damascus) was a visual one, but Jesus also spoke to Paul. Jesus met the disciples Cleopas and another unnamed disciple on the road to Emmaus and the disciples did not recognise Him at first. [4] Jesus only gradually became recognisable to them, although speaking to them for some time as they walked along the road. Jesus must have been different from the person He was during His life.

Jesus was also not subject to normal physical laws e.g. He appeared within a room with the doors being locked. [5] He could

---

[4] Luke 24:13 onwards
[5] John 20:19

appear very suddenly and also appear in different places for example Jerusalem and Galilee. [6] The partial physical nature of these appearances is rather puzzling. The only place on His body where it is recorded that the disciples actually touched Jesus was His feet. [7] And in another appearance, Jesus told Mary Magdalene not to touch Him, as He was not yet ascended to His Father. Were only the feet touchable? And how could He eat if He was not solid? Jesus broke bread and ate with His disciples. [8] Also, in two places in the Gospels, Jesus handled things, the bread in Luke 24 and the fish in John 21.

One important fact of the appearances of Jesus was that many people saw Him. In the upper room, ten disciples at one time saw Jesus. Paul records that 500 persons, both men and women saw Him at one time. Also saw Him. Thus, there were a large number of people who had known Jesus during His life who saw and recognised Him after His death.

One supposed parallel with the appearances of Jesus after his resurrection is the appearances of Mary, the mother of Jesus, to Bernadette Soubirous at Lourdes. On that occasion, although there was a large crowd present the only person who saw and spoke to Mary was Bernadette. In the same way Mary only appeared to the three children at Fatima, although a large crowd was present. On the other hand with the resurrection appearances of Jesus, there is no record of any disciple who was present at the time, who did not see Jesus. And what of the presence of Jesus where 500 people, both men and women saw Jesus. How could this be subjective? Interior visions do not happen to 500 people at once.

The appearances of Jesus are mysterious and cannot be explained fully. They are fragmentary and at the same time are too real to be explained away. These appearances are not just visual but are too unlike an ordinary human being to suppose that Jesus just revived in the tomb. It is just as if Jesus walked in from heaven and disappeared again back there. He also looked the same as He was previously, but He was also different. He said, "touch me not". Perhaps He was just like what we will be when we are in heaven Being who He was, Jesus could transcend the boundary between earth and heaven.

---

[6] Matthew 28:16
[7] Matthew 28:16
[8] Luke 24:28

Three conclusions about the Resurrection appearances of Jesus.

Firstly so far as critical historical research is concerned, the criticism seems to be very unhelpful. The historians have not found any direct parallels, so they just ignore 90% of the evidence, saying it all came from the authors. They have their own neat conclusions and too bad if the evidence does not fit.

Secondly, the appearances of Jesus were real and not interior visions or hallucinations. But these appearances were mysterious, without any other parallel.

Thirdly, we can say that Jesus did make brief appearances to His disciples and to Paul. These appearances took place in various places shortly after His crucifixion. We also know that the resurrected Jesus was definitely different from what He was during His life. He was not a resurrected body, but a completely different being, who was not subject to time and space.

The appearances of Jesus lay the foundations of a comprehensive doctrine of the hereafter. If you start with Jesus in heaven and the persons who believe in Him and who are also now in heaven with Him, you have the basis of Christian doctrine. There must also be some kind of future for those who did not listen to the warnings of Jesus and so you have a revised doctrine of hell. However a doctrine of hell was already found in Jewish beliefs. And Jesus promised to come again so there is the start of the doctrine of the Second Coming of Jesus.

Over the years, the Christian Church has developed the doctrines further so there is now a full doctrine of the hereafter, which can be stated in the paragraphs below.

The traditional doctrine of the hereafter

This doctrine has nine elements, which we will discuss at length. The nine elements are:

1) Temporal death, which is separation of the body from the soul or spirit.
2) The particular judgement, which God passes on the soul at death.
3) The intermediate state, which is the condition of the soul between judgement and the last day. The evidence for the existence of this state is given below. Vermena in his book "*The promise of the future*" tries to give a coherent account of the intermediate state, where dead Christians lie in a disembodied state, rather than go

direct to heaven (like the dying thief in the gospels). He bases this assertion on four main texts viz.
"Die and be with Christ" [9]
"All are made alive in Christ" [10]
"We will not be found naked" (verse 1) and "Heaven is a house not made with hands eternal in the heavens." [11]
"The spirits of the righteous made perfect" and "the assembly of the first born, who are enrolled in heaven." [12]
Are these texts sufficient evidence for a disembodied state? What are your views, Reader?
4) The Second Coming of Jesus Christ.
5) The universal restoration of the dead, both good and bad.
6) The general judgement at the last day (the Great Assize).
7) The end of the world or possibly the Universe.
8) Eternal life in heaven.
9) Eternal damnation in hell.

We shall consider each of these doctrines more fully in the next chapters. However there are many problems about this system. In particular it does not allow for the doctrine of the Communion of saints. It also has a very doubtful doctrine of the intermediate state.

The goal of our existence

We have to take into account two alternative accounts of the goal of our existence here and now on earth. These are the individual goal of existence and the communal goal of existence. These alternatives are a matter of faith or belief and are not subject to any kind of proof.

The first alternative goal of our individual existence is the belief of Christians, Jews and Muslims that we are destined for heaven or hell after death and that we shall live forever (or at least a long time) in the new sphere of existence.

The second alternative goal of our individual existence is the atheist idea that this life is all that there is and there is no hereafter. Choice of one of these goals must be made, as they are incompatible with each other.

The social goal of our existence partly follows from the individual goal and can be classed into three alternatives.

---

[9] Philippians 1:23
[10] 1 Corinthians 15:20-23
[11] 2 Corinthians 5:1-10.
[12] Hebrews 12:2-3

The first alternative is the belief of Jews, Christians and Moslems of the goal of a heaven on death and a partial heaven on earth now. This heaven will only be partially reached because of sin, but we have to work out what we can do to realise this goal. This is the action of healing the sick persons and caring for the poor and is partially happening just now. Of course that is tied in with a promise of heaven as well, which will happen one day in the future.

Secondly the Nazi or Marxist heaven goal of realising heaven on earth with no reference to religion. This goal could be classified as hell on earth rather than heaven on earth.

The Nazi goal was unashamedly racist. The future was heaven for some (the racially pure Aryans) and especially the torture and death for Jews and disabled and a slavery hell for Slavs and a constant surveillance for the rest of the population. The thousand-year Reich only lasted 13 years but in that time it did immense damage to humanity.

The Marxist goal was that you sacrificed everything now for a future, which was to be heaven on earth for the next generation. In practice it meant famine, torture, murder, informers (one-third of the East Germans were informers) for the population and unbelievable luxury for the leaders. The last vestige of this is North Korea today.

There is a third social goal of our existence and it is the technological paradise of the atheists with plenty for all and improved medicine to give freedom from disease and to give also to give people the life style that they demand. People do not wish any restraints. If they want children, then they must have them. If they want illegal drugs, then they must have them and ignore the consequences for others. They cannot accept what they have been given in life but must get what they want regardless of how it affects other human beings. The technological world has delivered many benefits, particularly freedom from starvation. There is plenty of food for all, if efforts were made to distribute this and shared it out fairly and put this into effect rather than the riches for a few. There have been tremendous advances in medicine (for which we are very grateful) and especially the use of antibiotics to control disease. But, the technological world has forgotten about SIN. Human desires are not always good and it could be a nightmare if all our desires were always fulfilled without regard to other people.

Chapter 6

HEAVEN

Introduction
The churchwarden was asked what would happen to him after his death. He said "I will immediately go into everlasting happiness, but I wish that you would not talk about such unpleasant happenings." What did he really believe heaven was like and why did he not wish to go there?

One hymn writer, Isaac Watts, described heaven as "a land of pure delight" where it is always day. Living there is a life full of pleasure without any pain. In heaven, the season is always springing and heaven is a place where everlasting flowers grow. This land is close to earth only separated from our present existence by death. This hymn gives a very pleasant view of what heaven is like and we must ask if this is a true account of heaven?

We are interested in the destiny of our relatives, our friends, and ourselves and as Christians, we would describe our destiny as going to heaven. This has been evident since New Testament times as the text below indicates.

"But we do not want you to be uninformed, brothers and sisters about those who have died, so that you may not grieve, as others do who have no hope. We believe that Jesus died and rose again: even so through Jesus, God will bring back with Him those who have died." [13]

There are two distinct sides to the idea of heaven. The first side is what happens to us after death, when we have the hope of being in heaven. Our individual destiny is a new person in a new existence in heaven.

The other side of our destiny is the future purpose of God for the world. "The faithful who are departed shall not be made perfect without us and so neither shall we be made perfect without them".[14] Heaven is not just an individual matter for any one person on their own, but a promise from God and is a corporate event involving our family, friends and other believers in Jesus.

St. Salvius, Bishop of Albi.
St. Salvius was believed dead of a fever, but he recovered consciousness. He described what had happened to him in the

---

[13] 1 Thessalonians 4:13-18
[14] Hebrews 11:40

intermediate period as being taken up by two angels and carried up into the height of heaven. He said that it was just as if he had beneath his feet not only the squalid earth, but also the sun and the moon, the clouds and stars. He was brought through a gate that was brighter than the light into a dwelling place where the entire floor shone like gold and silver. There was an inexpressible light and the place was indescribably vast. He was trying to describe a foretaste of heaven.

Historical Review
Biblical Ideas of Heaven

We have to consider six words used in the descriptions of heaven in the Bible, particularly in the New Testament. These words are Paradise, The Kingdom of God, Rest, Glory, Peace and Life.

1- Paradise.

Paradise is a Persian word used in Greek. Xenophon, who saw the garden of the Persian king in an expedition to Persia, first used the word in Greek. The word is found in the Greek version of the Old Testament. In Genesis 2:8 "the Lord planted a Paradise in Eden" (The Garden of Eden). The word is also found in Ecclesiastes 2:5 " I made myself gardens and parks and planted in them all kinds of fruit trees" and also in Lamentations 2:6 and in Song of Solomon 4:12. There is a similar text in Isaiah 31:3 "He will make the desert like the garden of the Lord".

The use of the word Paradise for describing the state of the righteous (Jews) in heaven is only found in Second Esdras (This book is found in some versions of the Bible) "the Paradise of delight." The word is also found in some other ancient Jewish books not in the Bible i.e. Enoch, the Testament of Levi and Second Baruch. This idea of the fate of the good Jews going to heaven is found only from the first Century BC. At that time, their Syrian rulers oppressed the Jews. A large number of faithful Jews were slaughtered for following their religion. There is a text confirming the belief in heaven from that time. "The king of the universe will raise us up to an everlasting renewal of life because we have died for His laws." [15]

The Jews believed that Paradise was a really wonderful place. They believed that in Paradise, there was abundance of all good things, healing of sick bodies and souls and happiness for all.

---

[15] 2 Maccabees 7:9

Paradise was a land where there were lovely trees such as frankincense, myrrh, mastic and nectar. Paradise was thus a garden, but more particularly a king's garden (like the gardens of Solomon and Artaxerxes). In the New Testament it was the garden of God. The various Jewish authors in New Testament times agreed that the Paradise of the Garden of Eden still existed, but disagreed about its locale in their own time. They also all agreed that it would return one day.

In the New Testament, there are only three instances of the word Paradise. The robber who was crucified with Jesus says "not only at the end, today you will be with me in Paradise." [16] David Powys explained away this text. His explanation was that Jesus was resurrected after three days, so the thief could not immediately have gone to heaven. But it is obvious that if Jesus was in heaven for the three days before returning to earth, then the thief could have gone to heaven on his death.

Paul, in Second Corinthians, [17] wrote, "I know that such a person was caught up into Paradise". In Revelation, John writes, "to everyone that conquers, I will give permission to eat from the tree of Life that is in the Paradise of God". [18]

2- **The Kingdom of God**

As well as Paradise, Jesus used the words "the Kingdom of God". This was developed from Jewish ideas and Christians used this phrase in the same way as the Jewish writers did, but applied the phrase to Christians instead of to righteous Jews. The word "inherit" was used in connection with the Kingdom.
There are three ideas here. The first was that the age to come contained the idea of God's kingship, in that He would be the heavenly ruler of that age. Secondly, the people of that Kingdom were all loyal to Him and there would be no rebels, i.e. no unrighteous persons would be in that Kingdom. Thirdly, a perfect life requires a perfect environment so there would be a new heaven and a new earth.

3- **Rest.**

Augustine wrote "There we shall rest and we shall see, we shall see and we shall love, we shall love and we shall praise. Behold what shall be in the end and what shall end."

---

[16] Luke 23:43
[17] 2 Corinthians 12 2-4
[18] Revelation 2:7

The idea of perfect rest also comes from the New Testament. The rest is that of the Sunday rest based on the promise of Jesus that you shall find rest for your soul.

4- Glory

Glory is an old word, not usually used in the context of the hereafter, but more usually used for achievement in this life especially sporting achievement. According to Chambers' dictionary, it has three meanings in the context of the hereafter.

The first is "the manifestation (appearance) of God to the blessed in heaven".

The second is "the presence of God."

The third is just another word for "heaven".

When people say or insert death notices in the paper "Gone to Glory", this just means gone to heaven or more especially going into the presence of God.

5- Peace.

"My peace I leave with you," said Jesus. Peace is peace with God, peace with Jesus, peace with other believers and as far as possible, peace with other human beings. It is often said that we shall find peace in heaven or that person (particularly the troubled souls who commit suicide), could not find peace on earth, but would at last find peace in heaven.

6- Life.

"But the righteous shall go away into eternal Life" [19] There is also the story told by Jesus of the young ruler who said, "what shall I do that I may inherit everlasting life". Jesus told him what to do i.e. sell his possessions and follow Him, but His advice was not accepted.

In the last judgement at the end of time, everlasting life is for those who have done well to people, who are the least of their fellow human beings. Paul also used the words "everlasting life for the future" and John declared everlasting life now. The Messiah had come in the person of Jesus.

Christians view going to heaven as going to eternal life. It is life, not death that Christians affirm. Although Christians mourn for dead people, they do so for themselves and because they miss that person, who is no longer with them on earth. They also want to show sympathy for the friends and relatives of the deceased

---

[19] Matthew 25:46

persons. However Christians do not mourn for the dead person, who has now gone to another life in heaven with Jesus.

The Greek view of the afterlife.

The Greeks did not view the afterlife as we view it. In one description of their beliefs, the Greeks had an idea of a soul entombed within the body. Death to the Greeks was the great liberator, as the soul was then free from the prison in which it was confined. Death loosened the chains that bound the soul to the body, and after the soul left the body, it could then go back to its eternal home. Even in Christian hymns we see something of this and the idea must be rejected. For the Greeks, death was a friend to be welcomed. For the Christian, following Jesus, death is an agonising process that is not willed by God. Death is an enemy, not a friend, even if it brings peace in a new life in heaven.

However this was not the only Greek view. The afterlife was a dark and gloomy place with no real existence, something akin to hell, as some people see it today. The shades were poor shadows of the human beings they once had been. This is indicated by the words of Odysseus in Homer's Odyssey. He spoke to the dead Achilles: "Formerly in your lifetime, we Argives (Greeks) used to honour you equally with the gods and now you are here and exercise great power over the dead. Do not grieve about it, Achilles, now that you are dead. Achilles answered "I would rather be a serf to a landless man, who has a small enough living for himself, than act as king over all these dead men who have perished."

The Christian view of heaven as a place of joy and real existence owes nothing to the Greeks.

Old Testament passages on Heaven

The idea of a future place for the righteous dead is only found in the latest books of the Old Testament, particularly in Daniel. It is also found in the books of Judith, Sirach and Wisdom, which are found in the Apocrypha. The writer of Sirach possibly implies the same beliefs as the other two books, but the author is more conservative than Judith and Wisdom.

However, some of the Psalms present the idea of heaven as a place for the righteous dead.
"For you do not give me up to Sheol,
Or let your faithful one see the pit,
You show me the path of life,
In your presence are fullness and joy,

In your right hand are pleasures for evermore". [20]
And the following text:
"But God will ransom my soul from the power of Sheol,
For He will receive us." [21]

Before the time of the latest Old Testament books, the belief was that the righteous Jewish dead went to Sheol, which was a place under the earth, where the dead, both good and bad dwelt. After the rebellion against the Syrians in the second century BC, the Jews thought that the righteous Jews would have a separate place where they would live forever. This place would be separate from the place where the unrighteous Jews went after death. (See the paragraph on Paradise) During the time of Jesus, there were two religious groups, the Pharisees who were the ordinary pious Jews and the Saducees, who were the priests. The Pharisees accepted belief in heaven, but the Sadducees did not believe in their resurrection after death. Jesus followed the belief of the Pharisees about heaven and the Apostles generally followed the belief of Jesus about heaven. However the Apostles applied the thought of the future resurrection to Christians instead of to the righteous Jews. The Apostles thought that Christians, who believed in Jesus, would have everlasting life after death. They believed that death could not separate them from Jesus and that they would be with Him forever.

New Testament passages on Heaven

The word for heaven in New Testament Greek has a variety of meanings. Like the French word for sky, which also has the meaning of heaven, heaven could just mean the sky. This is seen in phrases like "when heaven and earth pass away" [22] and "Clouds of heaven." [23] This is rather an exceptional use for the word "heaven" in the New Testament.

In some passages in the New Testament, the word "heaven," Lord of heaven" and "sinned against heaven" are just other names for God. This is easily seen if you make a substitution of the word God for heaven in these passages.

However, heaven has the third meaning of the unseen spiritual realm, which ancient authors thought was above the sky, but which, we might consider to be another dimension of the universe.

---

[20] Psalm 16:10 and 11
[21] Psalm 49:15
[22] Matthew 5:18 and Luke 16:17
[23] Mark 14:62

This unseen spiritual realm was also the dwelling place of God, as e.g. "Our Father in heaven." (Lord's Prayer), "heaven opened", "Heaven shut up," "angels in heaven," and "powers of heaven". There are also texts in the rest of the New Testament, where heaven also has the meaning of the dwelling place of God and Jesus. These are "remain in heaven" [24], "Paul caught up into the third heaven,"[25] "things in heaven" [26] "heavenly places", [27] "hope in heaven" [28] "citizenship of heaven", [29] "heavenly country",[30] "swear by heaven", (same as swear by God) [31] "kept in heaven" [32] and "heaven opened" [33].

The only descriptions of heaven are given in St. John's gospel where heaven has many resting-places and in the visions of St. John in Revelation. The visions in Revelation are not literal descriptions, but are imaginative ideas.

If we carefully look at these texts in the New Testament, readers can see for themselves that heaven and hell are closely associated with the New Testament and should be taken into account when considering a theology of the hereafter.

The majority of these New Testament passages does not say anything about heaven, but assume that it exists. Heaven is where God and Jesus are now. The ideas of many rooms in heaven, heaven as our home and also our citizenship of heaven, add to the brief statement of heaven's existence. But the mention of heaven in so many New Testament passages assures us that the belief in the existence of heaven cannot be easily set aside.

As well as direct texts with the word "heaven", there are other passages where heaven is mentioned under another name. These can be summarised as follows:

"Eternal Life" in John's gospel 23 times and in St. Paul's letters 9 times and also in St. Peter's letters.

"Eternal Salvation" [34] "Eternal Redemption" [35] "Eternal Inheritance"

---

[24] Acts 3:21
[25] 2 Corinthians 12:2-4
[26] Ephesians 1:10 and Colossians 1:10
[27] Ephesians 2:6
[28] Colossians 1:5
[29] Philippians 3:20
[30] Hebrews 11:13-16
[31] James 5:2
[32] 1 Peter 3:15
[33] Revelation 19:11
[34] Hebrews 5:9

[36] "Eternal Covenant "[37] "Eternal weight of Glory" [38] "Eternal glory" [39] "Eternal comfort and good hope"[40] "Eternal house not made with hands, eternal in the heavens" [41] "Eternal kingdom" [42] "Eternal gospel" [43] "What cannot be seen is eternal" [44]

Heaven cannot be ignored or explained away. It is clearly firmly established in the New Testament as the home of God and Jesus.

The Church Fathers and their description of heaven.

The nature of the resurrected body in heaven was controversial. Some of the fathers maintained that this body was a spiritual body, others maintained that the resurrected body was material. Some fathers even said that the atoms comprising the present bodies would be collected and would comprise our bodies in heaven. Some too, were influenced by the Greek doctrine of the immortality of the soul, which has found its way in to Jewish thought and is found in the Wisdom of Solomon.

The first and early second century fathers

These men were living just after the first apostles died. They are Clement of Rome (40-97), Ignatius (died 117), another Clement, Justin Martyr (110-165), Theophilus of Antioch (c168) and Irenaeus (135-200).

These writers see heaven as a reward or gift for believers in the risen Lord, martyrs, leaders and as a prize for good conduct. Irenaeus also said that the earthly body would be resurrected. He also explained that there would be different grades of beatitude, growth and advancement in heaven and finally communion with God.

The fathers of the third century

These writers had developed their ideas. They were Tertullian (160-230), Cyprian (c. 200-258) and Origen (c185-220). Tertullian

---

[35] Hebrews 9:12
[36] Hebrews 9:15
[37] Hebrews 13:20
[38] 2 Corinthians 4:17
[39] 2 Timothy 2:10 and 1 Peter 5:10
[40] 2 Thessalonians 2:16
[41] 2 Corinthians 5:1
[42] 2 Peter 1:11
[43] Revelation 14:16
[44] 2 Corinthians 4:18

and Cyprian added very little extra, although they put forward the idea of a perfect resurrection body free from sickness. Cyprian expressed the idea of a direct entrance to heaven after death. Origen had the idea of a waiting place for everyone before the resurrection. He also gave a description of the resurrected body, which would be a spiritual or glorified body, different from our material body, but would be recognisable. This body would have the same form as our present material body and would be the same in its interior state i.e. our intentions for good or bad. This body, too, would be a transformed version of our present body, being subtler, purer and more resplendent. Origen had the notion of spiritual development and growth in heaven. He thought that the kingdom of God as the contemplation of God in an ultimate truth and indescribable beauty. Origen was the first to propose the idea of everyone, both saints and sinners, going to heaven.

The fourth century fathers

These include Cyril of Jerusalem (315-386), Basil (c.330-379), Gregory Nazianzen (c.329-389), Gregory of Nyssa (c.331-396), Pachomius (died c.346), John Chrysostom (c.345-407), Cyril of Alexandria (died 444), Theodoret (393-457), Ambrose (c.340-379) and Jerome (340-420). We will consider Augustine (354-430) separately. There are five separate beliefs found in these writers

Firstly, the idea that everyone would go to heaven because of the resurrection of Jesus. (Following the work of Origen). People would need cleansing before going there (Gregory of Nyssa)

Secondly is the description of heaven, which would include knowledge of God, even if that knowledge were dim. The other idea is the identity of our present body to the resurrected body. The idea of heaven as a festival was common.

The third idea is of immediate entry into heaven with no intermediate state (especially Ambrose)

The fourth idea is that people now experience in this life a foretaste of their eternal destiny.

The fifth idea is meeting the saints in heaven.

Augustine came to the conclusion that no finite end can satisfy the human heart. He saw the vision of God as the chief of our desires. Augustine said that heaven has its own activity and praise. He thought that heaven had also different levels of happiness and that there would be no envy there, nor any discontent. Like others, he visualised the peace of heaven, where there was an ordered and harmonious life of those who enjoyed God and who were with one another in God. Heaven would be a city, where no friend left and where no enemy entered. In heaven, we were united in the everlasting love of Jesus. Augustine described what the risen body would e like. It was a spiritual body, not made of flesh and blood. None of the acts of the flesh would take place in heaven. There would not be any eating, or drinking nor having children in heaven. We would be like "the angels of God". Some of the church fathers believed in resurrection where the original particles of our body were reassembled in heaven, but Augustine stated that the risen body was a spiritual body, not made of flesh and blood. The risen body was incorruptible. He believed that our resurrection was a consequence of the resurrection of Jesus. Without the resurrection of Jesus, there would not be any resurrection for us.

Summary of the ideas of the church fathers.

Some of the ideas of these fathers are not unlike what we believe today, notable seeing God, friendship with one another and also joy in heaven. However some of the fathers had a mystical idea of heaven (this is not easy to explain, but means being very close to God). These different ideas of heaven, either as a lovely place or as being close to God or even becoming a part of God has been seen throughout the Christian era.

The fathers had also to try to describe what our bodies in heaven were like, without saying that they were just the same material as our present bodies. The also said that all our present bodies would be resurrected in heaven. On the other hand the fathers had also absorbed some of the ideas of the immortality of the soul from Greece and so they sometimes neglected the physical body. The Christian idea of the hereafter is the resurrection of the body rather than the immortality of the soul and the church fathers sometimes confused or amalgamated the two rather conflicting ideas.

Mediaeval ideas of Heaven

There are three main strands to the mediaeval idea of heaven, those of the contemplative, the mystic and the popular idea (such as held by common people and popular preaching).

Contemplative Heaven

The contemplative heaven can be seen most clearly in the theology of Thomas Aquinas. Aquinas was a monk and had a very static idea of heaven. His view of heaven only had one activity, which was contemplation. He thought that contemplation would provide us with an unsurpassable idea of God. Aquinas called this

idea of heaven attained by contemplation, the "Vision of the divine", and this was identical with what later theologians called the beatific vision. He thought that complete happiness could only be obtained in heaven, but this was because complete happiness could only be found with perfect knowledge, which could only be found in heaven. He said that love resulted from knowledge as "nothing is loved without being known". The measure of beatific knowledge depended on how much a person has loved God during their life.
Bonaventure, who was a monk, indicated that there would be love among the inhabitants of heaven. He said that true friendship was universal. He meant that there would be non-exclusive love among the heavenly dwellers. This idea equated love with friendship.
Thomas a Kempis said that plenty of people die quite suddenly without any warning. The Son of man would appear, just when we were not expecting Him.
Mystical Heaven.

The Pope, Benedict XII stated that the judgement at death admitted the soul to the Beatific Vision or Purgatory. But, the two important exponents of a mystical heaven were Mechtilde and Gertrude, who were beguines (a kind of nun, who were not necessarily in a convent for life). They saw heaven as a union with the Divine. This is explained more fully in the paragraph on mysticism.

Popular Mediaeval Heaven.

The general preaching of the monks and friars and the popular theology made heaven more like a pleasant earth. Heaven would have the attributes of the Garden of Eden. This took two forms the rural and the urban. The medieval rural idea was that heaven would be a green land with a temperate climate and plenty of flowers. The mediaeval urban idea of heaven would look like a mediaeval city, with all the attributes of an ideal city. This was not the urban squalor of a town in the Middle Ages, a town, which was a rather unpleasant place by our standards. We can think of any city in the Middle Ages. It was very dark, with no lighting. The stench of sewage in the streets was unimaginable to our noses and the city was a very unsafe place due to various thieves and murderers (much worse than today). There was however a number of people, who were not too badly off, and inside these houses of the better off, the city would not have seemed too bad. The heavenly city based on the mediaeval city would have a Gothic cathedral, celestial castles, golden streets; buildings decorated with precious jewels and richly dressed inhabitants.

In this city, lilies and roses would always bloom for you, smell sweet and never wither. Their fragrance never ceased to breathe eternal bliss into the soul. (Olfrid of Weissenberg) The inhabitants would have blessed the Lord through heavenly song and music. The mediaeval heaven would be dominated by religious concerns. The Church was the heavenly Jerusalem and the mediaeval city's buildings would reflect their view of heaven.

Just think of some of the hymns of this time describing the heaven as the New Jerusalem. Bernard of Cluny described heaven as a golden place, a place blessed with milk and honey and the home of god's elect (the Jews). And also another hymn by Peter Abelard describes the joy and glory, the crown (of victory, having reached heaven) and the rest of the weary ones.

The city or rural idea may seem like Paradise, but it was not only a perfect existence. The religious idea of heaven was not far from the thoughts of people in the Middle Ages. Heaven was the dear country, the happy home and the eternal rest. Heaven was nearness to God. If you lived in medieval Europe, you were living in a pious age when human thoughts were not far from God.

Poetical Heaven -Dante

Dante was not a theologian, but a politician and poet, who wrote an allegory about heaven, hell and purgatory. Dante described his visit to heaven accompanied by his childhood love, Beatrice, who died before him. Eventually Beatrice left Dante and for the final visions of heaven, Dante was accompanied by St. Bernard of Clairvaux and finally by the Virgin Mary. Dante described heaven in the same way as he described hell. This time, however heaven was made up of circles of light. Like the poem on the Inferno, Dante describes heaven in stages and described fully the people who lived there. The first circle of heaven held breakers of vows, an offence, which Dante did not consider serious. Then came lovers of glory followed by straight lovers, as Dante had a soft spot for lovers. The fourth level was the place where the theologians were. Higher up in heaven were the martyrs and Crusaders, followed, on the next level, by righteous rulers. (Dante had experience of unrighteous rulers). Still higher up in heaven, were the contemplatives. In Circle 8 there was the triumph of Christ and finally below the Trinity were the nine orders of angels. The Trinity sat at the top of heaven.
All this is not to be taken literally, but to be seen as a poem about heaven. Like the poem on hell in the Divine Comedy, the poem about heaven was not an allegory like Pilgrim's Progress, but a mixture of the allegorical and the projected fate of real people.

However Dante's description of heaven has never been surpassed and has greatly influenced views on heaven.

Reformers thought on Heaven.

Like everything else in religion, the Reformers changed the current views on heaven. Their idea of heaven was closeness to God. Ideas such as seeing friends and having heavenly happiness were jettisoned.

Victorian Heaven.

The Victorians had the idea of progress although the popular hymns still kept the idea of heavenly rest. The Victorians modelled heaven on their own ideas of life. The thoughts of the reformers were gone. Heaven was no longer a static place of rest but it was now a busy place with thoughts of progress.

Twentieth Century Heaven

The problem with the twentieth century idea of heaven is that there is a backlash from secularism and nineteenth century physics. Life on earth became much better for many people due to the advances of science. Belief in heaven and its location has declined because people are so attached to this world they cannot believe in another existence. Curiously, it all seems possible today that the essential self can exist in another dimension after the death of the person.

Heaven on Earth

Christian reformers for many years believed that it was imperative for Christians to improve the life of people here on earth. This was especially for the poor and downtrodden members of society. This can be seen in the movement to abolish slavery. While we cannot make heaven on earth (because of human sin) we can go some way to make the earth a better place.

Atheists took the idea of heaven on earth and developed it. Some of these beliefs are the Marxist heaven on earth, the National Socialist perfect racial heaven or the technological heaven on earth. None of these beliefs has worked in practice, and so the hope on living in a perfect earth has disappeared with these beliefs.

Ways to describe heaven

We cannot actually describe heaven as we can describe a person or object or place. We can only give a picture of it, according to what we believe comes closest to our ideal of heaven.

There have been several major insights into our idea of heaven. These are not mutually exclusive, but are just ways of trying to describe what is indescribable to us. These insights are:
The Beatific Vision.
Heaven as seeing family and friends.
Heaven as home.
Heaven as a beautiful place.
Joy and Heaven
Happiness and heaven
Our conscience and heaven

First, there is the **Beatific Vision**. It is the idea that we shall see God and we shall be forever with Him. (The dictionary definition is a glimpse of the glory of heaven.) The New Testament has three texts, which attest to the Beatific Vision. These are:
The words of Jesus "Blessed are the pure in heart for they will see God". [45]
The words of St. John "Beloved, we are God's children now; what we will be has not yet been revealed. What we do know is this: when he is revealed, we will be like him, for we see Him, as He is." [46]
And St. Paul said "For now we see in a mirror dimly, but then we will see face to face." [47]
Although we will see God face to face in heaven, we can only ever know a tiny part of God as He is. The Beatific Vision is seeing God in heaven, not having full knowledge of Him.

In this life, we can only have a very faint glimpse of what heaven is like and that is not by direct knowledge, but by looking at some things in our present existence and saying that heaven must be like that. Some people describe heaven as being able to "Hug God" or saying "when Jesus we see" like the words in the hymn.

However there are people called mystics who give a clearer picture of heaven. These mystics have been granted special insights into heaven. But all these insights are only a tiny, tiny glimpse of heaven. The mystics talk of being in union with the one (God). Some mystics have been contemplatives who have spent all their lives in prayer and meditation in a monastery or nunnery. But some have led busy lives. St. Thomas Aquinas was a very busy teacher and writer (the Summa Theologiae is published in 60 volumes, although it is incomplete) and was a person who travelled

---

[45] Matthew 5:8
[46] 1 John 3:2
[47] 1 Corinthians 13:12

widely in mediaeval times. Yet, just before his death, he had a vision and wrote no more saying that all he had seen made his writings seem like straw to him.

Possibly a more understandable mystic was Mechtilde of Hackeborn (died 1299). She and Gertrude both were responding to the male Jesus with mystical ideas of their own. Mechtilde saw Christ as a heavenly lover in the fashion of mediaeval courtly love. Courtly love was rather a love affair from afar, such as a knight would have for his lady, on whose behalf he jousted in the tournaments. The knight would have no contact with her, but love her from a distance. This is not unknown in our own time, with the love and admiration of girls for Hollywood actors and pop stars. This is love from a long way off and love with no danger of actual contact. Courtly love was similar to that. Mechtilde thought that heavenly union was similar to courtly love, where the beloved might receive caresses or kisses, but sexual union was not part of that love. However Mechtilde did not finally leave it at that, but eventually developed the idea of sexual union with Christ the King. Mechtilde's description of heaven involved a series of locations. The first heaven was a place similar to Paradise. The second heaven was filled with heavenly choirs. The third heaven was reserved for God and Jesus except that the purest of virgins could enter Christ's presence.

Another mediaeval mystic was Gertrude. She took the idea of heavenly union more literally as being a real union with Christ. She saw herself as Queen, who would have intercourse with the King. But both Mechtilde and Gertrude did not see union with Christ and themselves alone, but the union with Christ was with all the virgins. This has echoes today, for in some Catholic orders, nuns wear rings and are seen as brides of Christ.

While other Catholics, notably St. Bernard of Clairvaux saw the union of Christ with all saints; Mechthilde and Gertrude saw the union only with the purest virgins. Certainly St. Thomas Aquinas would have been horrified with the actual ideas of Mechthilde and Gertrude.

What are we to make of the mystics and their desire for heavenly Union with Christ? We must remember that there are mystics in other religions. Muslims too have their mystics. But mysticism can produce insights, which can act as a corrective to some of our very material views. We may desire more to see friends and relatives than to be with Jesus in heaven. But we must realise that heaven does involve both closeness to Jesus and also that we will see those whom we love in this world.

Secondly, Seeing and being with family and friends

We might also possibly meet people we did not know in our earthly lives but have heard of in Church or elsewhere e.g. St. Paul. Bereaved persons may want to see Jesus, but their minds are also on seeing lost loved ones, their families and friends and especially those lost so tragically in childhood, those murdered teenagers and those lost in wars or died at an early age. But it is not just in these tragic situations that we wish to see our loved ones again, for we have all lost someone we loved. And especially we long to see our parents once again. So the dead persons will need to be recognisable and not disembodied souls. The Christian idea, fully stated by St. Paul is that we would put on heavenly bodies. Origen thought that we would have bodies identical with those we had on earth.

St. Cyprian said "in heaven, our home, we have waiting for us a throng of persons who are dear to us; we have longing for us a vast number of parents, brothers, children, who already assured of their own immortality, are all still concerned for our salvation. What joy it will be for them and us, when one day we will find them again, and are able to draw near to them, see them, embrace them."

One of the most appealing pictures in art is the meeting of a family in heaven. (See art appendix) The artist can picture what we all perceive and what will happen when we arrive in heaven.

Thirdly, Heaven as Home

In many of the hymns we see heaven as home. These hymns can be found in most hymnbooks or alternatively in the Cyberhymnal on the Internet. The first hymn we could consider is by Thomas R Taylor "I'm but a stranger here, Heaven is my home." The next is a hymn by James Montgomery "Forever with the Lord". This is a hymn which describes a wanderer who is absent from God, pitching his tent every night, nearer his home in heaven. The third hymn we could consider is by De Witt C Huntingdon "O think of a home over there" and simply starts by thinking of a home in heaven. The fourth hymn by Alfred H Ackley "Jesus, I am coming home today where home is with Jesus and the fifth by Annie C Smith just starts "How far from home" (Home is heaven).

As well as whole hymns devoted to heaven; many hymns have single lines with the theme of heaven as home e.g.

"when Christ shall call me home".

Why does the idea of heaven as home have appeal? The main reason is that for many of us, home is associated with joy and happiness. We think of our homes here on Earth and think of the good times at home, either as children with our fathers and mothers or as adults in our own homes. It does not matter whether we are married or not and whether we have children or not, we love our homes. No matter our circumstances, we think of our secure base, which we call home. What better thought could be had about heaven, when we shall not only see Jesus our Friend, but also our own beloved family, which we knew here on earth? The hymn writers could not think of any better way to describe heaven than this.

Some of the hymns make the mistake that they equate Jerusalem as home. Good examples are "Jerusalem, my happy home" and "Jerusalem, the golden, with milk and honey blessed". John, who was a Jew from Israel, wrote his book The Revelation of St. John the Divine. This was written when John was in the prison on Patmos. He thought of Jerusalem with longing, but for us Jerusalem is a far off capital city. It was a Christian city when many of the hymns were written and as recently as the 1922 census was still a Christian city, but the Christians have long since emigrated. Jerusalem is not our home or anything like it.

We must think of home as what we enjoy here on earth and also what we might enjoy in the future and not some unknown far off city. Heaven as our home is a really beautiful thought.

Fourthly, **Heaven as a beautiful place.**
Heaven is Paradise. This is the lovely land of our future, where everything is perfect. The idea of Heaven as a beautiful place can also be found in hymns. A few examples are given below.
"There is a land of wondrous beauty". This hymn by C Austin Myles describes heaven as a place where "no flowers fade" and no summers perish." A hymn by Fanny Crosby reads "We sing of a land where the servants of God, Shall meet when their journey is o'er." The writer had hope that in heaven, she would walk with Jesus. This land (heaven) is described as a place "where the leaves never fall" "where the bloom never dies" and "of the friends who are waiting today". The writer had hope that there she would walk with Jesus.

Another hymn by Fanny Crosby is "We shall reach the summer land. "And from a hymn "In heavenly love abiding" by Anna Laetitia Waring heaven is described as a land of green pastures and bright skies which the writer had not seen. And another hymn already quoted by Isaac Watts describes heaven as a "There is a land of pure delight."

In another hymn by Thomas Alford "Ten thousand times ten thousand" states that in heaven, there will be restoration of severed friendships, no more partings and no orphans or widows. Another hymn "For those we love within the veil" by William Charter Piggott describes life in the world beyond. He describes heaven as the goal of human life, where there is no obstacle to seeing God's face. We would then know God's will and be able to serve Him. So wonderful is that life in heaven that we cannot conceive it.

To summarise the hymns about heaven, we could say that they talk of heaven as a wonderful place, so wonderful that anyone can scarcely describe it. But a writer cannot do justice to the magnificence of the hymn writer's vision and the wonderful works of God. The reader must read the hymns for himself or herself.

Some other thoughts on **Beauty and Heaven**

Just imagine that you are on the pier at St. Andrews. It is a perfect day. The sun is warm and there is hardly any breeze and you are protected against what breeze there is. There is no one else or just a single companion. It is quiet, except for the gently lapping waves. It is silent. Do you feel anything or sense another presence?

On a mountain pass in the Rocky Mountains, a man met a very old Roman Catholic priest. He was surprised to see him as the priest was very old and very weak and he asked the priest, "What are you doing here?" The old priest said I am seeking the beauty of the world. But, the man said, " surely you have left it very late"? The priest explained how he had lived all his life shut up in a cell. One night he had a vision; an angel came to him. "What have you come for" he asked the angel. "To lead you home", was the reply. "And", asked the priest "Is it a very beautiful world to which I go". "It is a very beautiful world from which you came," said the angel. "But I have seen very little of the world I am leaving" said the priest. Then the angel said "You will see very little beauty in the world to which you are going". The old man pled for time to see the world. He pled for just two years and two years were granted to him. "And now" He said, "I am spending all the money I have, and the little time that is left exploring the world's loveliness: and I find it very wonderful".

(Dr. Boreham)

Or you are up or halfway up a mountain or hill and you have a vista over rivers and hills, trees and fields. The scene seems so beautiful that it reveals the presence of the eternal.

Or perhaps you are in a garden with all the lovely colours, blues, pinks, reds yellows and white. God made such a diversity of colour and we can see His handiwork in all of this and is it not too a glimpse of heaven?

But there is also great beauty in the universe. The sun itself is very beautiful and the Corona is really a wonderful sight. And what words can describe the Aurora Borealis? And the magnificent sight of the stars and all that space is truly marvellous. Does that too, not give you a glimpse of heaven?

Fifthly, **JOY and Heaven**

There are some texts, which indicate heaven as a place of great joy. "Enter into the joy of the Lord." [48] "You may be glad with an exceeding joy." [49]

The joy of heaven is also found in the words of St. Bernard " In heaven, the reward is to see God, to live with God and to live in God. Where God is, the Good supreme, the happiness supreme, true freedom; there is true joy, perfect understanding, infinite beauty and beatitude" And in the words of St. Chrysostom, "Happiness is to know the people, who have loved on earth and to find them again." We have fleeting glimpses of great joy on this earth and so we will have greater joy in heaven.

Sixthly, **Happiness and heaven**

One old hymn by Andrew Young describes heaven by these words: "There is a happy land, Far, Far away" In the Imitation of Christ by St. Thomas a Kempis, we read of a poor beggar going into a magnificent palace (an analogy of heaven). The beggar learned that no one can complain of him, no one shall hinder him and nothing would stand in his way. The beggar found that everything he wished would be given to him. This is a view of the great happiness that will be with all of us in heaven.

Part of this happiness would be due to the absence of any suffering or sickness or pain. There would not be any hunger or thirst or cold or heat. There would be no more sorrow, because of the deaths of our loved ones. Our bodies would have eternal health.

---

[48] Matthew 25:21
[49] 1 Peter 4:13

In heaven, there would be no need for eating or drinking or sleeping. Our animal nature would not exist. St. Basil said that in heaven we would open out like flowers. And we would be friends with each other and with God.

Seventhly, **Our Conscience and Heaven**

In scene V of the play, *St. Joan* by Bernard Shaw, Joan had a conversation with the Dauphin (Charles). The Dauphin said to Joan 'Why don't the voices come to me. I am the king not you.' Joan said "They do come to you; but you do not hear them. You have not sat in the field in the evening listening for them. When the Angelus rings you cross yourself and have done with it; but if you prayed from your heart and listened to the thrilling of the bells in the air after they stopped ringing, you would hear the voices as well as I do.'

Are we like the Dauphin or like St Joan? Do we really hear voices? Are the promptings of your conscience not the voices of heaven? Do we sense heaven or the eternal, the presence of God? Perhaps the promptings of heaven may be unconscious, but they come. How often have you said you would do something out of the blue? Or did you decide not to go somewhere or travel on some train or make some car journey or be in some place that had a disastrous flood. Suppose, I had been on the train that collided in the Paddington rail disaster? Or if I had not had that phone call and was delayed on the road by ten minutes or caught in some of the floods, then I would be lying wounded in hospital or in heaven now". Do we sense heaven or the eternal, the presence of God?

Where have these ideas come from? Have they come from your inner self or externally or are they voices from heaven, whether you realise it or not? These ideas are not accidental; they are the voice of the eternal. God speaking to you.

On the night of the Tay Bridge disaster the story goes that a man from St. Andrews was travelling from St. Andrews to Dundee to go on the fatal train at St. Fort Station. He was delayed. He missed the train, which was an amazing coincidence. But did he really receive a message from heaven and unconsciously lost the train. What are coincidences? Are coincidences not the voices of God from heaven?

What is heaven like and do we have any possible glimmerings of heaven in this life?

As well as the descriptions of the beauty of this earth,

there are some other ways to describe heaven.

Music

Hildegard of Bingen (one of the first women composers) declared that music links human beings with God. Does a piece of music make you feel something? Does any particular hymn or say Handel's Hallelujah chorus make you feel something within yourself. Pavarotti said 'I don't think Mozart was a composer. He was a carrier, a messenger from God sent with music already written ". A musicologist said, "Handel had by some extraordinary feat drawn himself completely out of this world so that he believed he dwelt in the pastures of God." The late Fred Levison in his book (see list in Appendix) stated that Elgar professed that he plucked his music from the air as if it came from heaven.

Scent

What can move you like the perfume of some flowers, say some scented sweet peas or roses (especially some of the old varieties) or lavender? The scent is wonderful, but why do we call it heavenly? Is it just a figure of speech or is it really a touch of heaven on this earth?

Art

Artists can give us images of heaven, images which are not easily conveyed by words in the same way as musicians can do. There are various ways in which artists have portrayed heaven. These include drawings, pictures painted in watercolours, oil paintings, sculptures and woodcarvings. Heaven is often portrayed also in pictures of the last judgement where human beings ascend to heaven after the judgement. Although historians have discovered trends over the ages, particularly changes after the Reformation, the ways of describing heaven after the Reformation roughly corresponded to the previous descriptions of heaven. Painters usually focus exclusively on one of these elements of heaven or the last judgement.

A list of paintings, with brief descriptions, is found in Appendix 2. The list is not necessarily complete but is a pointer to what can be found describing heaven in art.

In some ways the pictures, which depict heaven are disappointing. We think of great Christian pictures such as the Last Supper, the Crucifixion and the Light of the World (William Holman Hunt) and we are disappointed with those pictures describing heaven. Artists have concentrated on

Biblical pictures, partly because they are trying to describe the Biblical message and partly because these pictures were useful educational tools in the past. The only other major religious theme portrayed, has been the Last Judgement. There are three types of pictures portraying heaven.

The first type is describing the Beatific Vision (i.e. a picture of God). This type of picture is heaven centered on God where we worship Him. One way of doing this is to portray light, which is coming from God. In these pictures the major figure or centrepiece is always God, Jesus or the Virgin Mary. Often it includes Christians looking at God or Jesus. These pictures often include angels surrounding God. A good example of this kind of picture is the blessed Damozel, where the Virgin Mary is at the centre of the picture. Another is the painting in the Cathedral of Torcello where the saints in heaven see Jesus. Francesco Russo paints heaven as light.

The second type of picture is the reunion of families in heaven. We really would like to see again our families, who went to heaven before us. While the saints think exclusively of being with Jesus, the rest of us expect both to see Jesus and to be re-united with our families. Also there various paintings show people being received into heaven e.g. St. Ignatius. Another theme is lovers being reunited in heaven.

The third type of picture is a picture of Paradise, which is often thought of as a kind of Garden of Eden. This is often a garden or a rural scene with fruit trees and flowering bushes. Sometimes heaven is pictured as a walled city.

However paintings directly picturing heaven are not the only type of art, where we may see what heaven is like. I can think of landscape paintings, which describe the natural world. As God is in this world, we should see His handiwork here, and also be able to describe or feel something of heaven in landscape paintings. As to modern art, I do not know enough to say what it describes. But in at least some traditional paintings, we can see heaven here on earth.

Architecture

As well as the beauty of art, so there is also beauty in buildings, although sometimes buildings are not beautiful. Why do have churches have high ceilings and lofty towering spires. Why do they have magnificent stained glass windows? The architects designed the churches and cathedrals not just for utility use, but to declare to us a message about the presence of God. The beauty of these buildings is there to lift up your minds above the daily concerns of life and to take your thoughts to heavenly things. Do not some of the modern Stalinist type buildings give a message saying something different (just the opposite message given by religious buildings) Their message is that here is ugliness so God does not exist.

Photography

Photography has moved on from just taking photographs of relatives, friends and snaps of holiday scenes. Besides actual events, photographers can use their imagination and photograph actual objects or scenes and use them as a picture of the next world. They do this by arranging objects or photographing scenes like a garden as pictorial illustrations of what heaven is like. Some photographs, which are found on the Internet and which describe heaven, are as follows:

1) "A very beautiful city". [50]
2) "An eternal day" (sun, sea and coast). [51]
This photograph comprises of an eternal Sabbath rest, a garden called Paradise (the Garden of Eden) a beautiful scene.
3) "A tropical scene with trees." [52]
4) "A new heaven and a new earth" (a rather weird picture) which is represented as a land with a living paradise of a garden. [53]
5) "A garden paradise" or a land with a living, garden paradise. (Like the previous picture) [54]
6) "Dwelling in God's very presence". (The most holy place in Jewish thought i.e. the Tabernacle in the desert, which symbolises the very presence of God.) [55]

Films

It is noticeable that some films have the theme of life after death. Some examples are given in Appendix 3. These films are not directly about heaven or the connection of Jesus to us when we go to heaven. They merely provide glimpses of what eternal life in heaven would be like. In church, the minister or priest tells a story. The story will be a lesson for us, but this story must also be

---

[50] Hebrews 11:16 and 13:14. Revelation 20:2 and Revelation 20:10 to 22:5
[51] Revelation 21:25 and 22:5.
[52] Hebrews 3:12 to 4:11 and Revelation 14:13.
[53] 2 Peter 3:3 to 3:13 and Revelation 21:1 and 21:5.
[54] Revelation 2:7 and 22:2-3.
[55] Hebrews 6:19 and 6:20 and Hebrews 9:11 and 9:24.

interesting in itself. In the same way, films must have an interesting story. Some films too, have a moral point. Many films are battles between good and evil, where the villain receives his or her reward in this life.

On the other hand, a very small number of films make a point about the existence of heaven. In Cocoon for instance, the viewers see old people being transported to another planet, where everything is wonderful. The old people will be physically renewed and have a wonderful life there. For that other planet substitute heaven, which, though it is not another planet, is another mode of existence. Other films show different aspects of heaven. Field of dreams, a lovely film, has a vision given to a farmer to make a baseball pitch in a field of maize. Famous baseball players come out of the field of maize to play a baseball game and supporters just come to see a game, which saves the farmer from bankruptcy. The players just walked out of the maize as if they had just come from heaven. Some films too, have persons coming back from heaven to right a wrong as for example "Ghost".

Not all of these films are directly about heaven but some films can reveal some thoughts about the after life and in particular, heaven.

Comic Strips

Comic strips can give some indication what is necessary for a person can enter heaven. A good example was "I'll see you in heaven, Leroy" (1971) Taken from the book "Heaven" (see list of books in the appendix)

Videos

"Hell and Heaven" This video shows scenes derived from the Book of Revelation. It is a fairly traditional description of heaven and hell.

Poetry and Literature

There are poetic images of heaven especially in Dante in his Paradise and in Paradise Regained by John Milton. But there are other poems, which would indicate a glimpse of heaven.

The old Anglo-Saxon poem The dream of the Rood has the following verses:
"When the young hero,
Who was mightiest God?
Strong and with steadfast mind,
Up to the Cross, with lingering steps he trod,
There to redeem mankind."
Does this too not indicate heaven?

What about Burns poem the Cottar's Saturday night. This poem indicates how a very poor working man and his family studied the Bible and prayed in his very little leisure time on a Saturday night. Is this not a foretaste of heaven?

There are other specifically religious poems such as Francis Thompson's "the hound of heaven". William Blake's poem "the blessed Damozel (where the lovers meet in heaven) is another poem about heaven. This subject was also painted by William Blake himself and by John Shaw.

But it is not just religious poems like these, but some of the poems concerning nature that could indicate heaven. A reader who studies the poem by William Wordsworth on the daffodils may also see a touch of heaven in the poem.

In Literature nothing can compare (outwith the Bible) to the Pilgrim's Progress by John Bunyan, where Christian and Faithful made their way through life, eventually arriving at heaven.

Tales of ghosts

There are many tales of unhappy ghosts. One story from Benvie (Angus) concerned the sightings of a white lady. The villagers were frightened when they saw her and so went to the minister. He approached her and asked what did she want? She replied that she had died of the plague. She was then buried in unconsecrated ground, and she wished to be buried in the churchyard. She promised that, if this was done, a well of water would appear and that this would be a cure for the plague. A well of water did appear and she was never seen again. Whether the water is a cure for the plague is unlikely to be tested now. These ghost stories (and there are many of them) together with the fiction of films are not proofs of heaven. But the stories indicate what Shakespeare said in one of his plays "There is more in heaven and earth, than is known in your philosophy."

Thin Places

Some places are described as thin places where heaven is apparently nearer. Iona has been so described. But in that place for so many centuries prayers have gone up to heaven. Is it any wonder it is so special a place for many? Another such place is Lourdes. In one book, a very cynical bus driver kept complaining about the visitors and the Church. But he said he loved the peace of the place. The reply was given to him. "You are a hypocrite. The peace, which you like, is not accidental. It is due to the prayers of the pilgrims over so many years". The peace here is due to the worship of God and that alone.

People
When you talk of saints you do not just mean the canonised saints of the Roman Catholic Church. All of the official saints are dead. We do not personally know the few, who lived recently like Mother Teresa. But often in ordinary people, you see something of likeness to Jesus. You have all met some one whose presence helps you. You feel a something about him or her. The presence of the eternal, which is the face of heaven, is there in that person.
Saints
The canonised saints were (the official saints are all dead) strange people, not really like us. One such saint was St. Teresa of Avila (already mentioned) who levitated. Several more recent saints have also levitated. Some examples are Joseph Benedict Cottolengo, St. John Bosco and Gemma Galgani. Other amazing feats of the saints include not eating or drinking. One example is Theresa Neumann who drank nothing from 1927 to 1962. Some saints e.g. Peter of Alcantara managed with a single hour of sleep per day for many years. But do these things not reveal that this present world is more different than we thought?

Another modern saint was Padre Pio. He had many strange attributes including the second man to bear the stigmata, which are the marks of the crucifixion on his body (the other was St. Francis of Assisi). He was reputed to be in two places at once. Padre Pio never left his cell. One story concerning him was that he spoke to General Carmona. The General lost the battle of Caporetto and he stood on the battlefield, contemplating suicide. He heard the voice of Padre Pio, saying to him "Don't do it". Many years later the General visited Padre Pio in his cell and the priest said to the General "You had a narrow escape my friend"

Another modern saint was John Vianney, the parish priest of Ars. He was so holy that he nor only influenced his parishioners, but could do marvellous things, particularly the miraculous multiplication of food for his orphanage. His influence on his parishioners in Ars was immense. The innkeepers of Ars moved away they did so little business and the village became quiet.

If we want a saint who is most unlike us is St. Joseph of Compostino. He was a lay brother in a monastery and was not considered intelligent enough to become a monk. His characteristic was to fly through the streets of Rome echoing shrill bird like cries. I wonder what the Romans thought of him? However due to his powers of levitation, he was considered a saint.

These saints had a wish to be very close to God. But their peculiarities make it very hard to consider that their view of heaven is the only complete one.

LIFE IN HEAVEN
What Will Happen To Us In Heaven?

There have been two ideas of what will happen in heaven, the static heaven and the dynamic heaven.

The **Static Heaven.**

This is the idea of heaven as eternal rest and eternal praise to God. It also includes the idea that at last we shall find peace for our minds. Rest is the dream of the overworked Victorian maid who would like to do nothing forever and ever. How tired she must have been, constantly running up and down stairs and with never ending work and being at the beck and call of the household from early morning until late at night. And she was allowed leisure on only a half day once a fortnight. But eternal rest is not everyone's ideal of everlasting happiness.

Peace

This is the idea of us at peace, rather than just at rest. We think of the relief of the tortured souls who committed suicide but are now at peace. Suicides in the past may have not been buried in hallowed ground but have been laid to rest outside the churchyard. But, we would nowadays adopt the Christian idea that the poor suicides are now at peace with Jesus. Their earthly life is over. We may miss them and regret that they have not made the most of their time here on earth, but they are at peace with Jesus where He is sure to welcome them and give that peace which He promised "My peace, I give to you".

The **dynamic heaven.**

We do not wish to be at rest all the time. Leisure is fine, but the idea of everlasting rest and possibly singing hymns all day forever does not appeal to all of us. We want to develop, see new things and do new things. Why should heaven be unending rest? We want to go on, to progress, to do things, to see relatives and friends and develop new interests, but at the same time we want to be free from earthly cares. And especially free from sin and wickedness. Two lines from the hymn "For those we love within the veil" by William C Piggott describes our life in heaven:

"Who knows to what high purpose Thou
Dost yet employ their ripened powers"

God has work for us to do even in heaven.

What will our bodies be like in heaven?
The idea of a post resurrection body was discussed in the chapter on the soul. The belief in resurrection to heaven is one of the questions about which there has been considerable debate. The New Testament is quite clear that the resurrected body is a glorified body and it is quite different from the body we know.

The Church fathers believed that God, by some mysterious process, would collect all the atoms together and recreate our physical bodies. But this is really just physical resurrection. Paul's view was that the relationship of our earthly body to our resurrected body was similar to that of a seed becoming a plant, which in appearance was quite unlike the seed. It is clear that this comparison must be not be pressed too far.

One theologian, Davies, thinks that Paul meant we needed to have bodily continuity but Paul just meant that the new body was quite different from the old one. Another theologian John McQuarrie discusses the question of a resurrection body. He tries (and I think succeeds) to answer the question of the continuity of our present memory and that of the memory in a resurrected body. He notes that the physical body, which we have at present, is not made up of pieces of matter (atoms and molecules) but is really energy. He states that some form of energy could constitute a link between our present physical body and a future resurrection body.

It is rather interesting that the idea of ourselves having a soul as well as a body is not too far from this idea of some form of continuity between this world and the next. McQuarrie also has another possibility of a resurrected body in heaven. He sees this soul or self as a pattern in time as a body is a pattern in space. He agrees with St. Thomas Aquinas that the self is a form of the body. While it is important to put a strong philosophical case for a resurrection body, which is in some kind of continuity with our present body, the exact details of its constitution and how it relates to time and space should be left to the future. Advances and physics will help us to formulate this more exactly. But remember that many atheistic critics of the thought of heaven are still firmly stuck in early nineteenth century physics. Perhaps new ideas in physics can help us to resurrect the belief in our destiny in heaven.

Our post resurrection bodies
These will be different from our present bodies. We read "He will transform the body of our humiliation (or our humble bodies) so

that it may be conformed to the body of his glory, by the power that makes all things subject to himself." [56] We will be recognisable as the same persons as we were on earth, but we will also be different. And we will have completely different characteristics. The first of these is impassability, which is incapable of suffering, pain or emotion. This is a wonderful thing. There will be no more sickness, or injury or weariness or sleep or hunger or thirst or cold or heat. There will be no more suffering sorrow or pain. Our new bodies will have eternal health.

According to St. Thomas Aquinas, we will have eternal youth in heaven. The men will have bodies of men of thirty years old and the women bodies of women of twenty years of age. We will be of one sex or other as there is no difficulty with being men or women. We will have the power of movement, of being able to appear or disappear and to go where we wish. Our bodies will be beautiful, but we will be as different from each other as we are on earth. The saints in heaven (ourselves) will not have the characteristics of their animal natures like eating, drinking, sleeping and sex. However the senses will retain their proper activities of sight, hearing, smell, taste and touch.

Do we go to heaven immediately after death or is there some intermediate stage?

There are several Biblical texts, which indicate that we will immediately go to heaven.
The dying thief who was told by Jesus "today I will see you in Paradise." [57]
The story of the rich man and Lazarus. [58]
Paul's wish to be with Jesus. [59]
Paul said "Absent from the body and present with the Lord" [60]
Paul said "And we are being transformed from one own likeness from glory to Glory." [61]

The church fathers thought of some kind of intermediate waiting state. As an example, Athenagoras said that the same bodies are given back to the same souls. Aquinas said that my soul is not I and that if only souls are saved then I am not saved, nor is any man.

---

[56] Philippians 3:21
[57] Luke 23:43
[58] Luke 16:22
[59] Philippians 1: 23.
[60] 2 Corinthians 5:8
[61] 2 Corinthians 3:18

The existence of the intermediate or disembodied state has several problems:
1) This does not agree with the New Testament teaching.
2) The possibility of a person existing without a body is a problem in itself.
3) The question of time is that already 2000 years have passed since Jesus lived. The world could exist for very many more years. Is the waiting period indefinite?
4) How can you square our time with time in the life beyond? If our future is beyond time, then the end of the world or universe, our immediate entry into heaven, the Last Judgement and the Second Coming of Jesus could all happen at same time or almost at the same time.
5) There are a number of philosophical and practical problems, including having an intermediate stage. H Price and his book "Survival and the idea of another world" has tried to make sense of the idea of a disembodied existence. He postulated the existence of another world, halfway between our material world and a dream world. This appears to be something like the future world of the mystics.

Conclusions
The chapter on heaven is made up of three parts.
The first part is a historical survey of what various Christians have thought about heaven through the ages.
The second part contains descriptions of heaven. We realise that heaven is about another dimension that any statement, which we can make about heaven, is provisional. Most of us believe that there are some glimmerings of what heaven is like in this life that, but these glimmerings are faint as life in heaven will be so unlike life on earth. We have looked beyond traditional theology to see what other subjects have to offer in the descriptions of heaven. Art, music photography, films and videos and even comic strips all have something to add, so that we have won greater understanding of what we believe about heaven.
The third part is life in heaven, either a static heaven or a dynamic heaven and we have discussed both options.

Concluding comment on chapter on Heaven
The words of John Donne, the poet, are as follows:
"The true joy of a of a good soul in this world is the very joy of heaven and we go thither not that we might have joy infused into us, but that as Christ says our joy may be full. For, as He promises

that no person shall take away our joy from us, so neither shall death itself take it away, nor as much as interrupt us, nor discontinue it. I shall have a joy that shall no more evaporate, than my soul shall evaporate. Joy shall pass up and put on a more glorious garment above and be a joy super-invested in glory".

Chapter 7

PURGATORY

As well as hell and heaven, mediaeval theology and current Roman Catholic theology has a third state, that of Purgatory. It is a place for unexpurgated penances (amends made for our sins, which were not made by the time of our deaths) and is really an intermediate state. When the penances expired, the inhabitants were destined for heaven.

The exact definition of purgatory is the state or place or condition in the "next world" between heaven and hell. This is a state of purifying suffering is for those who have died and need purification. This is a temporary place and in the end there will only be heaven or hell.

The Biblical basis for a belief in Purgatory is a text in 2 Maccabees.[62] This passage contains the story of Judas Maccabeus, who sent his men to collect the dead from a battle with the army of Gorgias (the Governor of Idumea). The dead men were found to have the sacred tokens of the idols of Jamnia under their tunics. This was idolatry, so Judas prayed to God to ask that their sin should be blotted out. As well as praying, Judas collected up an offering, which he sent to Jerusalem. The passage goes on to read "For if he were not expecting that those who had fallen would rise again, it would have been superfluous and foolish to pray for the dead. But if he was looking to the splendid reward that is laid up for those who fall asleep in godliness, it was a holy and pious thought. Therefore he made atonement for the dead, that they might be delivered from their sin".

However the biblical text is not the only justification for the doctrine of Purgatory. The Roman Catholic Church has held that Christian theology does not only depend on the Bible and its interpretation but also that Christians have insights under the influence of the Holy Spirit. (A good modern example is the Immaculate Conception of the Virgin Mary) Thus the doctrine of Purgatory came from reflection on Scripture under changing circumstances and it was not just obtained from a literal interpretation of a Biblical text.

Purgatory is a way of releasing people from hell. None of us are perfect (not even the saints) and we do not deserve heaven. We

---

[62] 2 Maccabees 12:39-45

need to be purified from our sins before we enter heaven and this purification is thought as being achieved in Purgatory. The most complete example of the doctrine of Purgatory is found in Dante's poem "Purgatory" which is part of the Divine Comedy.

The Church Fathers laid the foundations of this doctrine. Clement of Alexandria taught that souls would endure some sort of remedial fire. This was not an actual fire. Gregory of Nyssa wrote that the reality of sin and guilt in the person is such that it makes the divine attraction painful. The suffering that is the result is not because God wants pain, but because of the suffering entailed in the encounter between the love of God and our imperfect natures.

Although something like Purgatory had been in the minds of Christians for many years, the actual doctrine of Purgatory was first proclaimed in a letter from Pope Innocent IV in 1254 and later confirmed by the Second Council of Lyons and confirmed by the Council of Trent. The reformers did not confirm the doctrine of Purgatory, because the doctrine was not Biblically based, as the Reformers did not recognise 2 Maccabees as being a book of the Bible. There are no other texts to support the doctrine of purgatory, but sometimes, with tenuous justification, the text of Matthew 12:31 i.e. Blasphemy against the Spirit will not be forgiven" has been quoted in support of the doctrine. Also "the fire of judgement" in 1 Corinthians 3:12-15 has also been quoted in support of this doctrine.

One justification for the doctrine is that there are relationships, which do not end in death, between living and dead people. After all, we believe we will see relatives and friends in heaven. So Roman Catholics are encouraged to pray for the dead and are encouraged to perform good works on their behalf.
Not only did the reformers not accept the doctrine; they even forbade prayers for the dead. These prayers did not necessarily indicate that dead people were in purgatory. The most likely explanation given by Protestants, for the justification for praying for dead persons, is that these prayers are the combined prayers of living and dead people to God.

There are two main problems with the doctrine of Purgatory. There is only one Biblical text, if you accept 2 Maccabees as part of the Bible. However, that passage does not provide sufficient justification for the doctrine. The passage in 2 Maccabees seems at odds with the suffering, which is undergone in Purgatory as in 2 Maccabees there are prayers and an offering to Jerusalem, but no mention of future sufferings.

Secondly, there is the problem of theology as well. All Christians believe that Jesus performed, for all Christians, a once for all saving work. Our sins are wiped out, making us able to go to heaven, imperfect as we are. We may need further growth, but there is no need for an intermediate place of suffering.

Chapter 8

HELL

"How can ye escape the damnation of hell (Gehenna)?" [63]

Jonathan Edwards, the great American preacher, proclaimed in his sermon on hell the following words. "The world of misery, that lake of burning brimstone is extended abroad under you. There is the dreadful pit of the glowing flames of the wrath of God. There is hell's wide gaping mouth open: and you have nothing to stand upon nor any thing to take hold of; there is nothing between you and hell, but the air; is only the power and mere pleasure of God that holds you up." The sermon had a profound effect on his listeners. Many were reduced to tears.

There is an old Scots story of the people condemned to suffer in hell, speaking to God, saying, "Lord, Lord we didna ken" "Weel" said the Lord, "ye ken noo".

INTRODUCTION

Before we start to consider what hell is like, we must affirm the existence of hell. There are a large number of Biblical texts denoting hell, of which fifteen are the direct words of Jesus (see Appendix 1). If we take the Bible seriously, it can be assumed that there is a place or state that is called hell. Further we shall take it evident that hell contains persons. There is an article in *Life and Work,* the Church of Scotland magazine by Andrew McLellan stating that hell is empty. This is not found in any of the theological works quoted and no evidence is given for this statement.

The chapter dealing with hell will be developed in three parts. Firstly, we shall discuss briefly the ancient Greek view on hell, as taught by Plato.

Secondly we shall consider the Biblical background to hell and what the views on hell have been in the Church fathers and in particular Augustine. Augustine has made the traditional doctrine of hell, as we know it today. We shall then consider the mediaeval doctrine of hell.

Thirdly, we shall consider what hell could mean today and what the current views on hell are at present.

---

[63] Matthew 23:33

Hell in Plato's works.
Plato said " With regard to hell as God's judgement on you for doing evil distributive retributive justice is the ultimate law of the spiritual universe. And the soul, either by its own resolve or by the influence of the company it keeps, changes greatly in virtue or vice. Then if through Communion with Virtue Divine, the soul becomes pre-eminently virtuous. It is changed to a pre-eminent region, another and better region to which it is borne along a holy road. Whereas it changes in a contrary direction, then the change of its abode is also of a contrary kind. O boy, O lad, think yourself forgotten of the gods. Know that as you become more evil, you join the company of more evil souls. And, as you become better, you join the company of the better: and then, both in life and all that follows death, you will do and suffer exactly as it is meet you should, like gone to like. For this is a divine judgement which neither you, nor any other luckless lad, will ever boast of having escaped."

Biblical words denoting hell
Old Testament
The Old Testament word for hell is Sheol.
Sheol
The idea of hell, as a place where the dead remained, goes back to ancient times. This belief was not just held by the Jews, but was also held by other ancient peoples, particularly by the Egyptians, the Babylonians and the Greeks. The ancient Jews had the view that all the dead went to Sheol, but made no differentiation between the righteous and the unrighteous dead. Sheol was a gloomy place, where God could take action, but chose not to do so. Sheol, though, was a place of immortality, not annihilation. God just leaves those in Sheol alone. Later in Jewish history, in the book of Sirach (found in some Bibles e.g. Jerusalem Bible) we see that God takes action in Sheol itself, rewarding a man in the day of his death according to his ways. [64]

Sheol had certain characteristics:
1) A place of darkness. [65]
2) A place of silence. [66]
3) A place of forgetfulness. [67]

---

[64] Sirach 11:26
[65] Job 10:21 and 10:22 and Psalm 143:3
[66] Psalm 94:17 and Psalm 115:17
[67] Psalm 88:12

4) A place of separation from God. [68]
5) **A place without knowledge of what transpires on earth.** [69]

The belief that all the dead went to Sheol changed gradually and especially with the martyrs of the second century BC. Although there were probably previous traces in the Old Testament, the belief began that righteous Jews died and were resurrected to a happy world. In the book of Daniel we find the text "Many of those who sleep in the dust of the earth shall awake, some to everlasting life and some to shame and everlasting contempt." [70]

In the books of the Apocrypha, there are a number of texts, which refer to Hades (the word corresponding to the Hebrew Sheol). Hades was thought to be below the earth. A good example of a text, which refers to Hades, is "He heads down to Hades in the lowest regions of the earth".[71] Other texts refer to "the deep belly of Hades," [72] "I never went down into the deep, nor yet into Hades" [73] "My life was on the brink of Hades below."[74]

There was now the thought of deliverance from Hades. "The deliverance of the righteous" [75] and "He has rescued us from Hades." [76]

The belief came to be that the fate of the righteous Jews was not just a vague existence in Sheol or Hades. The idea that the good Jews were to be rescued from Sheol is found in these texts of the first and second centuries BC and this paved the way to a fuller belief in heaven and hell.

New Testament

The New Testament word for hell is Gehenna.

Gehenna

However, in the New Testament, a new concept of the hereafter came into being called Gehenna, which was a place for the unrighteous Jews. It took its name from a place called Gehenna now called the Valley of Hinnon, which is near Jerusalem. Gehenna is Hinnon in Hebrew, with the Hebrew letters rendered directly into

---

[68] Psalm 6:5
[69] Job 14:21
[70] Daniel 11:2
[71] Tobit 13:2
[72] Sirach 51:5
[73] 2 Esdras 4:8
[74] Sirach 51:6
[75] Wisdom 18:7
[76] Daniel 3:66 (Prayer of Azariah)

English. Gehenna was the place where Ahaz and Manasseh, the renegade kings of Judah, sacrificed children to the god Moloch. It was thus a place of utter abomination. Later it was supposed to be place where rubbish was dumped and set on fire. So we have the idea of a place of abomination together with destruction by fire. This made it a suitable place for the dead unrighteous Jews. In intertestamental times (between 400 BC and 4 AD), it became a place where, it was thought, unrighteous Jews would be punished with fire at the end of the world.

In Jesus time the word Gehenna was in common circulation in vague terms just as hell is today. Like the 19th century preachers, the word was used as a call to righteousness and avoiding sin. Jesus appears to have used the word as a call to righteousness. We must also remember that Jesus main message was about the Kingdom of God and that the subject of the fate of the unrighteous Jews was not His first concern. At the same time we must recognise that the word was used in the New Testament and none of our present day scholars know exactly what was meant by the word in the time of Jesus. Just as many people are not clear as to what is meant by hell today, even though the word is in common usage.

In the New Testament, the word is described as unquenchable fire and the opposite of life. The word Gehenna is used three times in Mark's gospel to denote that the hearers would be thrown into hell because of the stumbling blocks of hands, feet and eyes. [77] It is also used once in Luke's gospel "fear Him who has authority to cast into hell". [78] In Matthew's gospel it is mentioned three times. Firstly to the Pharisees, "You make the new convert twice as much a child of hell as yourselves" [79]. Secondly, "fear Him, who can destroy soul and body in hell. [80] Thirdly, How can you escape being sentenced to hell?" [81] In James' letter, [82] the tongue is set on fire by Gehenna.

Hades

The Greek word for Hell is Hades.

Hades is derived from the Greek view of the underworld. In its original form Hades was the god of the underworld, but later Hades was given as the name of the underworld. The use of the word in

---

[77] Mark 9:42-48
[78] Luke 12:5
[79] Matthew 23:15.
[80] Matthew 10:28
[81] Matthew 23:33
[82] James 3:6

the New Testament has nothing to do with its Greek origin, but is merely the most suitable word for translation of the Hebrew into Greek. The word is used as a translation of the Hebrew Sheol (which in Old Testament times was a place for receiving all the dead). Hades came to be used as a place for the wicked where they remained everlastingly or as a temporary place for all the dead.

Tartarus There is another Greek and New Testament word for hell called Tartarus.

For completeness we must mention the word Tartarus. It is found in 2 Peter [83] and nowhere else in the New Testament. The word is derived from Homer's Odyssey, and was the place where the Titans were chained for endless punishment. The original text concerned angels not men and the reason for use of the word here in uncertain.

Summary of Biblical words used

Hades and Gehenna were both used as words for the abode of the dead or for the place of final punishment for the wicked or for both the dead and the punishment of the wicked at the same time. Whether the use of one or the other is important is a subject for controversy by scholars, but it probably is of no great importance to us. It is very difficult to be certain of the exact differences between the words.

Hell in the Gospels

A list of the texts referring to hell in the New Testament is given in Appendix 1. These texts use the word Gehenna in all except two instances.

Jesus uses the word "hell" in fifteen instances, but six of these are parallel sayings in Mark and Luke. The sayings are really warnings about conduct and tell us very little about hell. Only the phrases "hell of fire" and "the destruction of body and soul in hell" tell us something about hell itself. The New Testament is very restrained compared with some later books about hell, the mediaeval doctrines of hell and the preaching of former generations of ministers.

There are parables and other phrases about hell as well as the actual word itself. These sayings have been classified into three

---

[83] 2 Peter 2:4

types. The classification is traditional and may be helpful to some people.

The first series of texts are **warnings** about what will happen to the audience of Jesus (often the disciples) if they persist with their current way of life. The threat of hell is used as a warning to change their behaviour. Jesus used symbols and parables e.g. the two debtors, the feast of the kingdom, the fruitless trees and the wheat and the chaff in order to warn the listeners of their possible fate.

The second group of texts is the message of the **rejection** or destruction of the hearers, if they do not hear the message of Jesus. These texts are all parables e.g. the man without wedding clothes, who was not allowed into the wedding.

The third series contains three texts, which are thought to be about **retribution**. Alternatively, these texts could be considered to be warnings to the listeners to change their lives. These three texts are the story of the rich man and Lazarus, the story of the unfaithful servants, who were punished according to their culpability and the parable of the sheep and the goats, which revealed the contrast between the fates of the righteous and the unrighteous.

The teaching of the gospel of St. John and the letters of St. John are about life. The texts indicate that God's gift of eternal life is only available through the work of Jesus. The gift of life is conditional and must be appreciated. This gift of life does not apply to the evildoers. These people could have a continual minimalist existence, which could not be called life.

Paul's epistles and Hell

Pauline texts indicate that Paul's main idea of human future was the wrath or the wrath of God (15 instances). Wrath is the righteous anger of God. This means that wrath is the consequence of human sin. If a person chooses to sin, this has consequences, which are the result of that sin. It is not God's punishment for sin, but is the result of God allowing us freedom to sin. Some theologians have seen wrath also as the fury of a Being offended by human sin. Sin is disobedience and is spelled out in detail in the epistles. [84] The consequences of God's anger may be in this world or the next.

---

[84] Romans 1:18 and Ephesians 5:6 and Colossians 3:6

Hell in the other New Testament books, James, 2 Peter and Revelation

The description of hell as eternal fire is found in James, 2 Peter and Revelation.

In James, "the tongue is itself set on fire by hell." [85] The text may indicate that the fire, which comes from hell itself, sets the entire course of our existence.

The text in 2 Peter "if God did not spare the angels when they sinned, but cast them into hell."[86]

Revelation has a number of texts referring to the final future of the wicked. They include the phrases "Keys of death and hell";[87] "There was a pale green horse. Its rider's name was death and hell (Hades) followed with him." [88] Death and hell delivered up the dead" and "death and hell were thrown into the lake of fire." [89] Again, these texts add very little to descriptions of hell, but would indicate that hell will not last forever.

Summary of descriptions of hell in the New Testament.

If we add together the three main descriptions of hell in the New Testament, which we have discussed in the preceding paragraph, i.e. fire in Revelation, outer darkness in Matthew and loss and separation from God in Mark, we have a strange composite picture. The main idea of these passages is that hell is associated with both fire and the outer darkness. There are two incompatible ideas being put together to make some kind of picture of awfulness.

What did the New Testament writers make of the fate of the wicked i.e. unbelievers? They said that they would be denied life and thus condemned to everlasting fire, judgement, and destruction.

There are just three texts, which may indicate the idea of punishment for the wicked and this does not include torture.

These are firstly, the story of the rich man and Lazarus, a story, which has many interpretations.

The second text is the fate of the unfaithful servant where the punishment seems to be more merciful than destruction.

---

[85] James 3:6
[86] 2 Peter 2:4
[87] Revelation 1:18
[88] Revelation 6:8.
[89] Revelation 20 13 and 14.

The third is the fate of those who did not give food or drink or a welcome to a stranger. [90] This refers to unending or eternal punishment, which could be destruction.

There is certainly not enough teaching in the New Testament to be the foundations for a doctrine of eternal torture, as was envisaged by Augustine.

The resurrection of the wicked.

There are three texts which state that the wicked will not simply be annihilated, but will be resurrected with a new body and face judgement and eventual punishment or extinction. These texts are as follows:

"Those who have done evil will rise to be condemned". [91]

"All people both good and bad will rise from the dead". [92]

"The lake is burning with fire and Sulphur, which is the second death". [93]

Too much stress must not be put on any text from Revelation, as many of the pictures in Revelation are symbolical and must not be taken too literally. However, the other two texts are too important to be ignored. The unbelievers too, will be resurrected after death, but their future will be hell and not heaven.

The Church Fathers and Hell.

The earliest Church fathers did not mention Hell.

The second century fathers, **Polycarp** (69-156), Ignatius (died 117), Justin Martyr (c110-165), Irenaeus (135-202), Tatian (died 180) and Tertullian (c10-230) all described the fire of judgement, an everlasting fire and everlasting judgement for the ungodly. When Tertullian was asked about the reason for this everlasting fire, he replied that the purpose of eternal judgement was to keep Christians from evil.

In the third century, Clement **of Alexandria.** (Died 220) and **Origen** (185-230) both reckoned that the purpose of the consuming fire, which was prepared for the wicked, because it was a spiritual or rational fire, which did not burn the flesh was to purify the soul. Origen believed in the ultimate salvation of every soul.

In the fourth century, **Gregory of Nazianzus** (c.329-389) wondered whether eternal punishment was worthy of God. **Gregory**

---

[90] Matthew 25:41 and 46.
[91] John 5:29
[92] Acts 24:15
[93] Revelation 21:8

of Nyssa (c.331-396) envisaged the eventual purification of the wicked, the disappearance of evil and the final restoration of all things. He said that the soul, having a natural affinity to God, must eventually return to God. He had rather an optimistic view and (like Origen) thought that all would eventually be saved. But personal purification was necessary and this would entail fearful torment. The torment would be incomparable to anything in this world, but the motive would be purification rather than judicial retribution. It would be something similar to notions of purgatory in the mediaeval Church. **Jerome** (340-420) made a distinction between the impious, who would have torture without remission and sinners, who trusted in God, and who would eventually be saved.

Augustine (354-430) was more severe and talked of unending torment as a consequence of human sinfulness. He fully accepted retributive punishment as a consequence of divine sovereignty. He allowed pardon in the world to come for people who were Christians at heart and who would be saved after undergoing purification in Purgatory. He said that beyond punishment, there would be alienation from the life of God, which would be the greatest punishment. The work of Augustine can be summed up in his thoughts of the two cities, the city of God where God rules and the city of darkness where the devil reigns over eternal punishment.

Other theologians of the fourth century, **John Chrysostom** (345-407) said there would be double divine retribution, once at death and once at resurrection time. **Hilary of Arles** (died 367) stated that the wicked would pay the penalty.

Some later churchmen continued Augustine's tradition, notably the **Venerable Bede** (673-735), who had visions of Hell and **St. John Damascene** (c.700-754) who denied repentance after death.

Mediaeval doctrine of Hell

The Divine Comedy written by Dante. Dante did not describe a literal hell, but an allegory of the individual's soul's journey through hell. He described the various states of persons in hell according to their sins. Dante did not really believe hell ran from Jerusalem into the centre of the earth, but in his allegory, he had to place hell somewhere.

Accompanied by Virgil, a pagan who could not go to heaven but was forever to remain in Limbo, Dante wandered hell, starting on Good Friday (then April 8). He divided hell into ten places (circles) and the various sins of the damned grew more serious as they descended deeper into hell. Leaving aside the Vestibule to hell, where the futile (those who could not make up their minds about heaven or hell) remained, the first circle was Limbo where the unbaptised and righteous pagans dwelt (something similar to the biblical Sheol). There was no punishment there.

The rest of hell contained the places where various sinners went, according to the gravity of their sins. The second layer of hell was the abode of the lustful where there was mutual indulgence and which Dante did not consider to be a serious sin, as this sin was unselfish and did not hurt others. The third circle of hell was the home of the gluttonous whose greedy appetite was entirely selfish. The fourth circle contained the dwelling of the hoarders and the spendthrift. When we go deeper into hell, the fifth level contained the wrathful persons and the heretics in level six. In between there is a layer of burning sand containing the blasphemous. Level seven contains the violent people in three concentric rings. The first concentric ring contained people, who were violent against their neighbours and also tyrants. The next concentric ring contained people, who were violent against themselves (the wood of suicides) and in the remaining concentric ring, those people who were violent against nature (the sodomites and maybe the present day drug takers). This ring also contained those who were violent against art (the usurers who made money breed interest, which was condemned in the Middle Ages).

The eighth concentric circle was made up of a number of layers. In order of increasing seriousness, there were simple fraudsters, panderers and seducers, flatterers, simoniacs, (that was a person who sold church offices e.g. bishoprics to anyone who came up with the money and included Popes Boniface VIII and Nicholas III). Others in this circle were sorcerers, barrators (i.e. those who traffic in public offices, maybe today the equivalent of politicians who secure jobs for their families). Others were hypocrites, thieves (we make look on thieving slightly more kindly, but in the Middle Ages theft was against the person and the thieves made no distinction between me and mine). Some others in this circle were counsellors of frauds (those who consulted with others to practice fraud (just think of the dishonest lawyers of our own day). Others were sowers of discord which could be either religious strife (Mohammed), civil strife (think of our modern day terrorists), or family strife (Dante quotes several notorious cases of his own time) and falsifiers, both ordinary falsifiers (perhaps false labelling in our own day) and falsifiers of metals (in our own time forgers of bank notes). The bottom layers were confined to traitors to their kindred, traitors to their country (just think of the Communist traitors who spied against their own country) and also traitors to their guests (imagining murdering your guest). At the very bottom were the traitors to their lords: Judas against Jesus and Brutus and Cassius against their country (The Roman Empire). Punishment was doled out according to their sin, except in Limbo where the persons were not of course sinners.

Sometimes we would think Dante was wrong. He was very unsympathetic to suicides, which we would say should not have been placed there. He was also very much against Pope Celestine V, who resigned from the Papacy, not surprisingly, as he was 80 when he was appointed and who later became a saint.

Dante does not give us a literal description of hell and the poem should be described as partly an allegory, similar to Pilgrim's Progress. However it was not quite an allegory, as many actual people were mentioned. These people were mostly from Dante's own time but also came from classical authors, both real and mythical. It is this reference to actual people, which makes the poem so authentic and supplies as good a description of the theology of the Middle Ages as we could find. The poem does indicate the seriousness of our sins and describes the reality of evil and the importance of making confession for our sins to God. The picture of hell portrayed in the Divine Comedy is a snapshot of the theology of hell in the Middle Ages.

Thomas Aquinas (1225-1274) said that guilt and punishment correspond to each other.

The subject of hell was popular in the Middle Ages and there are numerous writings on the subject.

The Reformers and hell

Because of the corruption of the doctrine of purgatory due to the sale of indulgences (certificates for the absolution of sins), the Reformers decided to abolish the doctrine of purgatory. The doctrine was also viewed to be wrong. If Christ saved absolutely and entirely, the idea of a further satisfaction, needed by existing for some time in purgatory, was not required. However, this decision placed a great divide between the good persons destined for heaven and the bad sinners destined for hell. This made a greater division of good and bad people than when it was believed that most people would have their sins expiated in purgatory. **Martin Luther** believed in hell, but also made a statement that he did not limit the time of acquiring faith to the present life. **John Calvin** believed in divine vengeance and the wretched conditions of the wicked. He believed in eternal fire, but said that it was a metaphor.

Calvin adopted the doctrine of the elect (people specially chosen by God to be destined for heaven). The main teaching of this doctrine was that only the elect would go to heaven and no one else. While Calvin thought that the workings of divine providence was a mystery, many of the Calvinists thought that the choice of the elect was a fixed (determinist) system, where the personal choice and the motives of any human did not matter. This doctrine of the elect too, had its disadvantages. If the elect were destined for heaven, then there was a danger that people, who were destined for heaven, neglected the necessity of obeying the moral law. There was also the danger that most people were now destined for hell, whereas in the Catholic scheme most people were destined for purgatory and so eventually heaven.

The Victorians and hell

Because of the extravagant sermons of many preachers, where the tortures of hell were explained in great detail, many Christians did not believe in hell at all. It did not help missionary work that these sermons were not believed. Various ways to mitigate the tortures of hell were proposed. One belief was the Universalist idea where all sinners would be saved eventually and hell was only temporary. As in all ages, there was a tension between individual salvation and the future destiny of the universe. However this was particularly important in the very individualistic outlook of the nineteenth century.

We have to beware that what ordinary Christians believe and what theologians say can sometimes be very different. However some examples are perhaps relevant. While John Henry Newman and Charles Spurgeon believed in a very literal hell and preached that doctrine, some other theologians had different ideas. As examples we take the following three theologians.

Friedrich Schleiermacher (1768-1834) believed that the power of redemption would result in a future general restoration of human souls.

Frederick William Farrar (1831-1903) said there was room for repentance beyond the grave. Some souls may be lost because they resist God forever.

Samuel Cox (1826-1893) said that the redemption of Christ extends to the life to come.

There was a new emphasis on personal believers and in particular salvation from sin and not salvation from punishment.

Twentieth Century views on hell
 Belief in hell in its classical form has declined since the Victorian era. The twentieth century theologians are generally split between the believers in eternal punishment, those who believe in eventual heaven for everyone and those who believe that unrepentant sinners will eventually be annihilated. Some clearer thinkers are listed below.
Emil Brunner (1889-1966) stated that no one could resist God. An eternal hell meant that the sacrifice of Jesus was an incomplete victory.
Reinhold Niebuhr (1892-1971) said that we do not know the temperature of hell. He indicated that we must not go into detail about hell, as we do not know the details.
Nicholas Berdyaev (1874-1948) said that belief in hell makes real life meaningless. We must believe in God because of our love for Him and not from fear of hell. Hell has been inflicted on humans.

WHAT IS HELL LIKE? WAYS TO DESCRIBE HELL NOW
The Brochure.
 You get a brochure form a travel agent to pick your exotic holiday. You see a beautiful hotel with pictures of swimming pools, palm trees and beautiful beaches. You choose your holiday and fly there. You may find the pictures are near reality or perhaps they bear no resemblance to the brochure. You discover that the Holiday Company has taken the pictures somewhere else and faked the whole brochure. The hotel turns out to be a nightmare of a building site, the kitchen of the hotel is full of cockroaches and the food tastes awful. Is hell like that? You and I have not been there. We depend on the brochure, that is the New Testament and especially the words of Jesus, who has actually been in heaven.

 What is the truth about hell? We depend on a picture, based on present reality. If heaven and hell were totally unlike Earth, we would not know what to say about them. We must construct pictures of hell very carefully or else say nothing. But we do have some clues as to what that future reality is like.

 We believe and have always believed that what any person does in this life counts very much. Our present life is a time of testing and preparation for the life to come. If you want eternal life in the future then this depend on how you live your life now. If you live it in fellowship with God, then you will have eternal life in heaven. It does matter what you do and what your life is like and whether you believe in God and wish to do His will. And it matters not just for the present, but for all eternity.

Gloom

Hell may be a gloomy place. A good example was found in C S Lewis' book, the Lion, the Witch and the Wardrobe. In his book, Lewis described the imaginary country, Narnia as a place where it was always winter, but never Christmas. This is a good description of hell as there is. Lewis described the small animals, which lived in Narnia and which were also always in fear of the wicked Queen. The Queen in the book could be another description of Satan.

Lack of beauty

One way to describe hell is by looking at Stalinist architecture. The monstrous 20th century blocks of Stalinist architecture in the grey housing schemes of Moscow (and elsewhere) reflect the atheist values. If hell is to be compared to anything in our world, it must be compared to life in these blocks, which are an unending dullness and greyness. The housing schemes with long platforms giving access to each door and the flimsy doors themselves give a sense of insecurity and lack of privacy. The fear of being mugged along these dark and gloomy corridors can give us a foretaste of what hell is like. The picture is complete with abandoned and burned out cars and graffiti everywhere. The text over the gates of hell (in Dante's Inferno) is "Abandon hope all ye who enter here" could apply to these housing schemes.

Even in the countryside you find this absence of beauty. There is a problem in the arable counties of Eastern England. The lack of trees and bushes, which were all, bulldozed out in the 1960's to make bigger fields and a single crop, which is wheat. And the point of this absence of hedges was just to save money, by making the task of sowing and harvesting the crop slightly more quickly. The absence of birds, which depended upon insects feeding on weeds in the wheat crop, is noticeable and we miss the vanished hedgerows. The farm workers too, have departed long ago. They migrated to the towns, as many of their jobs were gone in the simplified farming systems. The countryside can give a picture of hell on earth.

And the long motorways crammed with cars are essential to our life today, but they create a picture of hell just the same. And the long lanes of static traffic just after an accident or even where there is some remedial work on the road surface can be described as a hell on earth for the unfortunate drivers.

Some of our towns, especially where the local council has neglected areas, can be a living hell. The heaps of rubbish, the discarded crisp packets, the lack of paint, the discarded syringes and the vandalised toilets are a picture of what hell could be like.

Discord not harmony.
All music is not good music to many people. Not everyone likes Scottish dance music or the latest pop music. Not everyone likes Beethoven's sonatas. But just think of the agony of listening to a poor player or a beginner on an instrument! And even worse is the agony of listening to loudly played rock music late at night to a music lover who does not like rock bands.

Hate not love.
Just think of the problems of hate in this world. The hatred stirred up against paedophile or suspected paedophiles or those who look like known paedophiles. There cannot be any excuse for known paedophiles, but think of the hate against innocent families who are accused of being paedophiles without evidence. Also hate is not a Christian attribute and having hate for others belongs to hell and not heaven. Think of the hatred in Northern Ireland, a hated stirred up by selfish people for their own ends. Think of the Nazis theme of hate for Communists, Jews and Slavs. Think of the Serbs and the Albanians who now hate each other, where before the Kosovo war there was some goodwill and tolerance and acceptance of each other.

Meaninglessness.
A grey world with endless rain seems to make the world devoid of meaning. An everlasting boring sermon is without meaning to some of the congregation. It is said that some of the nineteenth century clergy came to the end of the time on their hourglass and felt that they had more to say they turned it over for another hour. A non-football lover at a football match wonders if the wretched match will ever come to an end. The miserable boring television programme with comics without humour is totally without meaning. These party political broadcasts are surely the worst five minutes you can spend. Even an empty boring job can be meaningless. One worker, who was applying for a job in Britain with a motor manufacturer, said that he worked for Ford in Detroit. He was asked what his job had been he said "I was nut and bolt number 203". Can there be any worse job than that?

There are places where God appears to be absent. Just as there are thin places where God seems near so there are places in this world where God seems very far away. Can you think of our prisons? The ever-persuasive smell of a prison, which is just a warehouse for humans, is particularly vile. This is the smell of slopping out, a lavatorial smell, which is persistent, disgusting and horrible. Bunyan may have been able to write Pilgrim's Progress in prison, but for most of us prisons are awful places.

But fire is not the only legitimate picture of hell. The Bible gives several pictures of hell, not just everlasting fire. Perhaps the best picture is that of dark places. We have an instinctive fear of the dark. Just think how much we enjoy the brighter nights. There is a condition called SAD where the lack of light in the winter affects people seriously. We long for the long days and short nights of spring and summer. This is the extent of our fear of darkness. Is it any wonder how hell is depicted as darkness as well as fire?
The loss and separation from God is an indicator of hell. God is in hell, just as He is everywhere, but we would feel His absence. Just think how desolate we are when we lose someone who is very dear to us. We are distraught. The picture of abandonment is a very powerful one. And how much more can being abandoned by God affect us!

Indicators of Hell in Art

Artists have created pictures of hell both in mediaeval and modern times. Most of the pictures are traditional, showing people being tortured by demons There are several examples of traditional and modern pictures of hell, and these are listed in Appendix 2. The list is not exhaustive. The pictures of hell, like those of heaven, are listed to show how some of artists have viewed hell. Many of these pictures are not oil paintings or watercolours, but frescos in churches or wooden pictures. Note that many pictures of hell were part of a larger picture of the Last Judgement.

Modern art is more difficult to comprehend. It has become fragmented and there is no one way that modern artists follow. One modern school of art is primitive, which is taken from the art of the Africans and the South American Indians, who use its masks and symbols which are repeated over and over again. Children's art is also primitive art. The Mediaeval artists were very careful in painting their figures and the objects even although some of the scenes were open to interpretation. Modern primitive art is deliberately careless, especially when it tries to imitate children's art. And yet it can also indicate hell if we study these pictures.

Indicators of hell in photography

Just as in the photographs describing heaven, we can also describe hell, using photographs. This method of description is a very modern technique and it also involves the use of a person's imagination. Some of these modern photographs, derived from the Internet are as follows:

Hell is shown as a picture of Gehenna (the Valley of Hinnon) as it is today. As this was literally the garbage dump of Jerusalem, so there are two ways to show this in photography. One way is to show the place as it is now, the valley of Hinnon, which is a barren place of rocks and bare soil and the only vegetation is a few bushes. The other way is to take a picture of an actual garbage dump in Jerusalem at the present time. [94]

Hell can be pictured as an eternal night. This eternal night is represented by a photograph of two eyes in a black background. [95] Another way to describe hell is "beaten and tortured while shackled in prison." The pictures are of an arm shackled. [96]

Hell can also be represented as "an act of destruction of a former time". (e.g. a picture of destruction like the ruin of Sodom and Gomorrah) This destruction is shown by a photograph of fire with smoke coming off. [97]

Hell can be photographed as a lake of fire and brimstone. This is simply a photo of lava in a volcano. [98]

Hell is imagined as "being exiled and banished away from God's kingdom and His very presence". As this is difficult to photograph, a drawing showing Pharaoh telling the Israelites to go. Pharaoh is drawn as a symbol for God. [99]

Hell is sketched as being consumed by maggots in a fire. This is easily shown by a large-scale photograph of a maggot. [100]

---

[94] Matthew 5:22 and 29 and 30, Matthew 10:28, Matthew 18:8 and 9, Matthew 23:15 and 33, Mark 9:43 and 45 and 47, Luke 12:5 and James 3:6.
[95] Matthew 22:13 and 25:30, Jude 13 and 2 Peter 2:17.
[96] Matthew 18:34 and 24:51, Luke 12:47 and 22:13.
[97] Matthew 3:12 Matthew 25:41 and 13:42, Jude 7, Mark 9:43 and 45 and 47, Mark 18:8 and 9, and Luke 3:17.
[98] Revelation 19:20, 20:10 and 21:8.
[99] Matthew 22:13 and 24:51, Luke 13:27, 2 Thessalonians 1:9 and Revelation 22:15.
[100] Mark 9:48.

Hell is drawn as a fire burning in an igloo. Again this is difficult to photograph without melting the igloo, but is easy to sketch.
Hell is thought of as a furnace of fire. [101]

Hell and Films

There are not many films denoting hell. However the two films which are listed below in Appendix 3 give some indication of hell. One is a time warp, where the same event happens over and over again, until the main character has a change of heart.

SEVEN VIEWS ON HELL

These seven views are annihilation, destruction, everlasting punishment, everlasting torture, punishment but with a future in heaven (or Universalism) a vague existence forever and purification.

Firstly, **Extinction or Annihilation**

This is what the atheists think will happen to them and is a possible view of hell. Atheists believe that this life is all there is and that at death, they will be totally annihilated. They believe that their bodies will be dissolved into their constituent parts, and that these parts will be reused, similar to plants in a compost heap. They also believe that there is no such thing as mind or soul or spirit. They believe that we are just electro-mechanical objects, which are no different from the computers we use.

The ancient Greeks said that annihilation was intolerable. They preferred Hades to extinction. This was a quite different attitude to that of modern atheists, who welcome the idea of extinction. The absence of eternity is a real possibility for the atheists.

However attractive to atheists, the idea of there being no life after death, has no Biblical basis and is contrary to two New Testament texts in John and Acts as well as one in Revelation, where the unbelievers are resurrected to eternal death. So the idea has to be ruled out by Christians. It is however the belief of the Jehovah Witnesses. The Witnesses believe that Sheol and Hades should be translated as the grave and that the fire of Gehenna is a symbol for annihilation.

There is also the idea that some unrepentant people would suffer a period of punishment and then be annihilated. But annihilation undermines morality. If there is no future punishment in

---

[101] Matthew 13:42 to 50 and Mark 3:12.

hell or reward in heaven, then how you live in this life does not matter.

Secondly, **Destruction**

There is no mention of extinction in the Bible. Instead, there is the idea of destruction, which is quite different in that people live after death, but their future is to be destroyed eventually. The main texts in the New Testament which indicate destruction, are as follows:

"You that are accursed, depart from me into the eternal fire, prepared for the devil and his angels." [102]

"These will suffer the punishment of eternal destruction, separated from the presence of God and the glory of His might. " [103]

Destruction takes place after the soul is in hell and could come after a long time there. Perhaps, most of the characteristics of human beings would be destroyed, leaving just the shadows of former human beings. This resembles the thought of the ancient Jews and Greeks where the souls went to Hades and were just shadows of their former selves.

Destruction is the consequence of disbelief in God and Jesus. It may be a possible alternative to hell or being in hell may be the same as destruction. This appears to be the general nature of New Testament teaching.

Thirdly, **everlasting or eternal punishment**

The dictionary gives the meaning of eternal as "without end", "everlastingly", "seemingly endless" and other definitions. We must first consider the question does hell last forever?

Is Hell Eternal?

There is a problem of the word "eternal". The Greek word which is translated eternal, does not mean eternal as "lasting forever", but "pertaining to the age", which may come to an end and often refers to "the age to come" and does not refer to our present existence. The Greek word for eternity also has a meaning of space as well as time. But when we think of heaven and hell, we are going beyond space and time. The word "eternal" could fill a whole book with its interpretations. When it is applied to heaven (51 times in the New Testament) it means lasting forever. It would also seem to be interpreted as lasting for a long time in the New Testament texts on hell. This can be seen in the following texts. These texts are

---

[102] Matthew 25:41.
[103] 2 Thessalonians 1:7-10.

"eternal fire" or "punished by eternal fire" [104] and "eternal destruction." [105]

But often in the Old Testament, (the word is found 70 times in the Greek translation of the Old Testament) eternal has a temporary meaning, for example the leprosy of Gehazi was eternal, but it eventually disappeared. Another example is in "And you shall take an awl and thrust it through his earlobe into the door and he shall be your servant for ever." [106] And another text is "And Achish trusted David, thinking he has made himself utterly abhorrent to his people Israel: therefore he shall always be my servant." [107] These texts using the word for hell are obviously not for ever, but only for the servant's lifetime.

Eternal refers to the age to come in the New Testament. The word not only refers to time and space, but also has a quality aspect. This is not unknown to us as we have the expression "quality time". Frederick D Maurice, a prominent nineteenth century Anglican, thought that the New Testament word for eternal referred to quality rather than duration of time. He was expelled from his position at King's College, but denied being an Universalist.

The whole subject of the word for eternity or everlasting has been a battleground between various thoughts of what lies beyond death. If any clear conclusions are to be drawn from the definition of this word, it would appear that eternal punishment means that the punishment would last for a long time, but it is not clear from the Biblical texts that it would last forever. And that really throws the question of any possibility of further repentance and salvation after death to be an open question with no really clear answer.

This view of hell as eternal punishment is not well attested in the New Testament, being only found in 2 Peter and Jude. The two rather contrasting themes of punishment are fire and darkness, which are rather two incompatible pictures. It can be necessary to give two incompatible pictures as the only way to describe a truth, which here is to picture hell in its awfulness. However, everlasting punishment has been the orthodox position since the time of Augustine.

Everlasting pain is found in both Augustine and Aquinas. Aquinas said that the pain in hell was not so great, and that it could be borne. This is not the view of modern day cartoonists, which

---

[104] Matthew 18:8, Matthew 25:41 and 25:46 and Jude 7
[105] 2 Thessalonians 1:9.
[106] Deuteronomy 15:15
[107] 1 Samuel 27:12

have rather devastating pictures of humans being roasted by the Devil. This picture is based on the belief that God's justice depends on the idea that sinners would be punished. It is the view, which is found in the poetry of Dante, where Virgil took him on a tour of hell. The preaching of eighteenth and nineteenth preachers also emphasised the terrible tortures of hell.

There is a difference between punishment and torture. Punishment may be that the individual is not fit for heaven now, but is destined for a lesser and not as pleasant a place and the individual would also be separate from Jesus.

Fourthly, **everlasting torture.**

The Biblical justification for painful punishment or even torture in hell is not very convincing. The main text for everlasting torture is found in Judith. [108] " The Lord Almighty will take vengeance on them in the day of judgement, To put fire and worms in their flesh, And they shall weep and feel their pain forever." However as a sole justification for everlasting conscious torture, this text does not provide sufficient justification for the belief. Like the doctrine of purgatory, the sole clear text is in the Apocrypha and this would seem an inadequate Biblical basis for a belief in torture. However some of the parables, for example the parable of Abraham and Lazarus might provide some justification to substantiate this belief, depending on how these parables are interpreted.

There is a modern book with a vision of hell, which has no biblical basis, but I am sure it was written with good intentions. The vision is one by Mary Baxter (See book list), which related to a tour of hell, given by Jesus. In hell, people are suffering, and are being tortured by demons. The book may serve as a warning to people to be righteous. And the book may even cause some persons to accept forgiveness for their sins.

Fifthly, **punishment with a future in heaven and universal redemption.** Universalism or Universal salvation or Conditional salvation

This is not a Biblical concept, but is greatly favoured by modern liberal churchmen. This picture of punishment as a prelude to salvation makes hell as an intermediate place with eventual redemption and our final destiny with God in heaven. Universal

---

[108] Judith 16:17:

salvation needs a section on its own and this will be given after the section on purification.

Sixthly, a **vague existence forever.**

This was the Old Testament view (of Sheol) as a place where all the dead, both the righteous dead and the unrighteous dead, went. This could be considered to be the same as destruction. This is not the Christian view, because our future in heaven depends on being resurrected by God and not on some idea of human immortality.

Seventhly, **purification.**

There are two texts in the New Testament where persons are purified by fire:

"The genuineness of your faith, though perishable is being tested by fire" [109]

"The fire will test what sort of work is done". [110]

Fire can be a symbol of destruction or it can be a symbol of purification as metals are often purified by fire. The belief that purification could happen after death and allow someone to enter heaven, when they would not otherwise be fit to go there, is similar to purgatory, but there are considerable differences. Purgatory is for Christians, while purification could be for anyone. Purification fits in with an Universalist belief of hell.

Universalism is discussed in the following pages.

UNIVERSALISM or UNIVERSAL SALVATION

Universalism is the belief that Christians and possibly some other people, would go to straight to heaven after death, but all the others, who were not saved, would go to hell for a period but not for ever. At some point, possibly after the Second Coming of Jesus, those people would eventually go to heaven. Thus, hell would be a place of purification and there would be further opportunities to repent. This makes hell similar to the Roman Catholic Purgatory. There are big differences between purgatory and hell, as only Christians can go to purgatory, but the belief in the existence of purgatory lessens the gap between the two destinations. However, the idea of further opportunities for repentance after death is similar whether the individual is going to purgatory or to hell. Universalism

---

[109] 1 Peter 1:7
[110] 1 Corinthians 3: 13 -15

is based on the fact that sin and wrath are temporary, as God's wrath and punishment are aimed at the salvation of all people. Wenham says, "in the end love will win its free and full response." There are objections to this idea, although it seems rather attractive to some at the present time. If this life is the one and only opportunity for salvation, this makes the decisions taken in this life more urgent. To many kind-hearted people the idea of hell for all eternity seems repulsive.

Jesus is supposed to have visited hell, between His death and resurrection. In the words of the Apostles creed (the main creed used by the Christian church) "He descended into hell". However these words were not part of the original Apostles Creed, but first were found in the fourth formula of Sirmium (359 AD.) The reason for this belief was that the early Church Fathers had great regard for the Patriarchs (Abraham and Moses). They thought that the patriarchs needed and deserved to be saved and that Jesus did this work between His death and resurrection. But fanciful as this is, and there is a good case for rejecting this addition to the Apostles Creed in favour of the original version of the Apostles Creed or the Nicene Creed (another important statement of belief) both of which do not make this assumption. However, there is some truth in this assumption. Even persons in hell are not beyond the love of God. It is possible that sinners persevere in their hatred against God so that they cannot accept God's offer of salvation. Even after death, they cannot tolerate God's presence and prefer hell to heaven. C S Lewis said that the damned enjoy an abominable black presence in hell.

There are several arguments for universal salvation

Firstly, there is the belief in the saving work of Jesus on the cross. An encyclical from Pope John Paul II says, "every person without exception has been redeemed by Christ, because, with every person without exception, Christ is in a way united, even when man is unaware of it". This encyclical is an accord with the Biblical teaching that the work of Jesus on the Cross, is a finished work and effective for every one of us. This is true for Christians but it is also true for Jews and Mohammedans, who also believe in God.

New Testament passages quoted in favour of universal salvation.

"Hallowed be Thy name." The Lord's prayer itself has some hope for universal salvation. So long as any sinner remains, God's name is not being hallowed. His Kingdom will not be complete until all are in it. There has also the parable of the leaven. [111] The yeast (which is the Christians and the faithful non-Christians) was mixed with three measures of flour (which is the unrighteous) until all are leavened. This would indicate hope for the wicked.

"God our Saviour, who desires everyone to be saved." [112]

"The Lord is patient with you, not wanting any to perish, but all to come to repentance." [113]

" Jesus, who must remain in heaven until the time of universal restoration that God has announced." [114]

"And I, when I am lifted up from the earth will draw all people to Myself." [115]

"For God has imprisoned all in disobedience so that He may be merciful to all." [116]

"In Christ, God was reconciling the world to Himself." [117] This means that as God is reconciling the world to Himself, that must include everyone in the world is reconciled to God, so everyone is with Him in heaven eventually.

"Through Him, God was pleased to reconcile to Himself all things, whether on earth or in heaven, by making peace through the blood of His cross." [118]

"When all things are subject to Him, so that God may be all in all." [119]

"The fullness of Him (Christ) who fills all in all." [120]

"And every tongue confess that Jesus Christ is Lord." [121]

"Jesus gave Himself as a ransom for us all." [122]

"God wills that all be saved. " [123]

"Son is heir to all things." [124]

---

[111] Luke 13:20
[112] 1 Timothy 2:4
[113] 2 Peter 3:9
[114] Acts 3:21
[115] John 12:32.
[116] Romans11: 32
[117] 2 Corinthians 5:19
[118] Colossians 1:20.
[119] 1 Corinthians 15:24-28.
[120] Ephesians 1:23.
[121] Philippians 2:11
[122] 1 Timothy 2:1
[123] 1 Timothy 2:4.
[124] Hebrews 1:2.

"Saviour of the world." [125]

The first argument for universal salvation is taken from the New Testament and depends on the texts quoted above. Are the above texts sufficient to support a belief that everyone eventually will be with Jesus in heaven? However nowhere is there any indication that all will be saved immediately after their death and go to heaven at their deaths. The hope of eventual universal salvation is very much different from that. The hope is that after the end of the universe and when a new universe comes into existence, then there is a possibility everyone will take that place in a perfect universe. However this doctrine does not say that going to hell after death is impossible, but just that those in hell will not be destroyed and will not be there forever.

The second argument is individual. This argument is often quoted as "A good God would not send anyone to hell." It is the individual idea that God is love. He will not let any person perish at the final day of Judgement, let alone suffer everlasting punishment. God is also omnipotent, so He will eventually save every one of us. The believers in Universalism take God's love for us and His omnipotence and add these together to obtain this result. The question here is not about God's love for us but does His omnipotence save everyone without compromising human freedom.

The third idea is the community idea that God is perfect, therefore the universe will be perfect. If there were any sinner who survived as a sinner then the universe would not be perfect. You cannot have sin within a perfect universe. And if the sinner survived outside the universe, then the universe (which is all that there is) would not be the universe. There is the question, that if hell is another dimension, then is it in the universe or not?

A fourth argument is that a just God would not give infinite punishment for finite sin. There are two answers to that statement. One is that sin is serious and has infinite consequences. The other is that hell is not just a punishment, but is the consequence of what we have become during our lives. If we are very bad persons, we are not fit for heaven, nor would we wish to be there.

Church fathers and Universal salvation

Most of the church fathers would have rejected universal salvation. However, Origen, in the third century believed in

---

[125] John 4:43 and 1 John 4:14.

universal salvation. Origen was considered orthodox in his lifetime. However, he was condemned as a heretic by the Emperor Justinian at the Fifth Ecumenical Council in 553 A D. This was three centuries after Origen's death. We must also remember in fairness to Origen that only 16 out of 291 commentaries still exist and only three of his letters exist, so we cannot take a proper view of what he taught. Most of what we know of his thoughts are from his opponents after he died

Modern arguments for universal salvation

Friedrich Scheiermacher (1768-1834) was an Universalist. He gave three arguments for the Universalist position.

Firstly he believed that the words of Jesus were all figurative in the following texts:
"These will go away into eternal punishment," [126]
"Than have two feet and be thrown into hell," [127]
"Those who have done evil to the resurrection of condemnation. " [128]

Secondly, there is a passage in Paul's letter to the Corinthians that "all evil shall be overcome." [129]

Thirdly, misery cannot increase, but must decrease. Thus the sinners in hell must grow less wretched.

Fourthly, the sympathy (and prayers) of the redeemed in heaven must save the lost.

Arguments against Universal Salvation

There are a number of arguments against the belief of universal Salvation.

Firstly, there are no passages in the Bible, which would definitely prove Universalism, even if the passages, which are listed above, can be quoted in support. We must always remember that if you hunt carefully, it is easy to find possible supporting arguments in the Bible for many beliefs.

Secondly, if we cannot eventually resist God's saving love, what does this do to the concept of human beings being free to accept or reject the Gospel. God's love for us cannot be at the expense of human freedom, as that would make human beings robots and not persons.

---

[126] Matthew 25:46
[127] Mark 9:44
[128] John 5:29
[129] 1 Corinthians 15:25 and 26.

Thirdly what does eventual salvation for all do to God's justice and human morality? Why should humans be moral persons, if it does not really finally matter what we do? Why give to Christian Aid rather than spend money on ourselves? Why not rob a bank, or even beat up pensioners for their money?

Some people today would deny the reality of sin. Sin is a very bad word today. The fear of hell prevents people doing what they like to do, when that thing is wrong. But although it seems very attractive to pretend sin does not exist, in reality it does exist and is serious. If anyone does not believe this, just read any of the daily newspapers. According to Origen, "Christ remains and the Cross as long as one sinner remains in hell" God loves His creatures with an infinite love and desires nothing more than their salvation. But this love demands a human response to Him. His love continues rejection and exists forever. Piers Ploughman in his poem wrote as follows: "Who suffers more than God". We can think of analogies in our world of a person's love, where the person still loves another despite continual rejection. Does only human love continue to love in spite of rejection? How much more than human love is the love of God!

It is really inconceivable a loving God would let people suffer eternally without forgiveness and without any means of alleviating their lot. The idea of punishment without the motive of revenge is attractive, but in the past punishment has been associated with vengeance on those who have been evil and who have committed horrendous wicked deeds.

Summary of the idea of Universalism

The idea of eternal punishment from God seems fair and just and it is often repeated that God is a God of justice. But He is not just a God of justice: He is a God of love. And it has often been stated that hell could also be a place of purification so that many more could enter into heaven. Salvation after death would also allow further opportunities to repent. Universal salvation makes hell similar to the Roman Catholic doctrine of Purgatory. This idea is rejected by the Protestant Churches because it has no direct Biblical basis. Some churchmen thought that there is a possibility that there is room for repentance beyond death. Frederick William Farrar (1831-1903) took this view, but also stated that some souls might resist God forever and that they would remain in an endless hell.

It is difficult to give a fair summary of the idea of universal salvation. The Biblical texts are both for and against the idea of

eventual salvation for all. But the two great arguments can be summarised below.
FOR universal salvation
The clearly expressed idea in the Bible, that the sacrifice of Jesus is the saving works for all human beings.
Against universal salvation
The warnings in the New Testament.
The majority of Christian teaching through the ages.
Conclusion
It is up to you, the reader, to make up your own mind.

SELECTED FOR HELL

Are you abandoned in Hell?
But the dead persons, who are now in hell, are not forgotten. St. Catherine of Genoa said "The sweet goodness of God shows His mercy even in hell". If you are in hell, you are not completely abandoned. God is there with you, waiting on you to recognise Him and accept Him. As the Psalmist said "If you descend into the depths of hell, I am there."

Who is going to Hell?
The question on which former generations of preachers have concentrated is who will go to hell and who will go to heaven. This can still be heard today, but not in church sermons. Frequently you hear the statement that he or she is on the road to hell. Phrases about hell abound. As an example we say that the road to hell is paved with good intentions. Hell occurs frequently in our conversations except in church. At one time, particularly in the Victorian era, the preacher could say to his congregation that they would be going to hell, unless they repented from their sins. The possibility of hell was also presented as a future for members of other denominations, particularly the Roman Catholic Church. Hell fire was reckoned to be the subject of a rousing sermon.

But there really is a proper question. If hell is a serious option for ourselves after death rather than immediate extinction, are some of us condemned to hell or is there another option? Jesus said believe in Me. If we really believe in Jesus and accept His sacrifice and forgiveness, then we shall definitely be going to heaven after we die. In the same way we can be said to be with Jesus now. For those who don't believe, but have heard the Christian message and rejected it, there appears to be only one option and this is judgement followed by a period in hell. Hell does not mean torture, but is a loss of a life in heaven.

The problem of those who never heard of Jesus can be solved if we accept that they will be judged according to their thoughts or works. And what about those who profess to be Christians but do such wicked things? One example of those people are child molesters, who profess to believe in Jesus, but do not obey His commandments. Only God knows what is in their hearts. Perhaps they do not truly believe, but take the opportunity to go into a privileged position where they have the opportunity to do evil. We see in the Divine Comedy how wicked popes, (who only loved power and money) were languishing in the lower regions of hell. We must not judge other human beings, but we know that for the wicked (but we must not personally identify them in case we are mistaken) then hell is their future. If we believe in the Bible, then all will not be saved at death, but we must never say that you, an individual, will not be saved. After all, Christianity is the good news of salvation, not the destruction of our neighbours.

Predestination Election and Freewill.
The meaning of predestination is that God has decreed from the beginning of time that the fate of a person is fixed for all eternity and that the destination of a person after death is either life in heaven or damnation in hell. The opposing doctrine is that humans are free to accept or refuse the offer of salvation and this is called free will. The two doctrines have been discussed throughout the Christian era.
Historical
The beginnings of the doctrine of predestination are found as might be expected in the New Testament and in two texts of the letters of St. Paul. The two texts are as follows:
"Whom He proclaimed, He also called: and those whom He called He also justified: and those whom He justified He also glorified." [130]
"For He destined us for adoption through Jesus according to the good pleasure of His will." [131]
The doctrine was given shape by St. Augustine of Hippo. He refined the earlier doctrines. Aquinas confirmed the doctrine of predestination and it was adopted in its severest form by Calvin and so passed into Presbyterianism and is confirmed in the Westminster Confession of Faith (The statement of the Christian faith devised by the Reformers). The founders of Methodism,

---

[130] Romans 8:29.
[131] Ephesians 1:5.

Wesley and Whitfield, also debated predestination and Whitfield founded the Calvinist Methodist Church to uphold the doctrine.
The eighteenth century in Scotland gave us two extreme examples and these are found in certain of the poems of Rabbie Burns and in the book *Confessions of a justified Sinner* by James Hogg.

We can quote a single verse of one of Rabbie Burns' poems Holy Willie's prayer as an example of the idea that we are selected from birth to go to heaven or hell after death.
The first verses of the poem are as follows:
"O Thou who in the Heavens dost dwell,
And as it pleases best thysel,
Sends ane to Heaven and ten to Hell,
A' for Thy glory,
And no for any good or ill,
They've dune afore thee."

Burns gave this account of Predestination in the above verses of his poem. Holy Willie understood that he was one of the elect and was destined for salvation i.e. if he died he would go to heaven. He prided himself on his good life, except when he was drunk when he did some bad deeds, things that he would not do when sober.
But Holy Willie was not really a good person, or he would have known to avoid being drunk and so not being led into temptation.
So Burns is making a mockery of a hypocrite, who only pretends to be good.

Burns raises many interesting questions. There are three main points:

Firstly, Burns states that 9% of us is destined for heaven and 91% for hell. The arithmetic is that of a poet who needs to fit rhymes into his verse, not that of a statistician or a theologian. But the point he is making that he believed that there are very few who are going to heaven. There will be further discussion on this point. How few will go to heaven is the debatable point. The gospels write, "Many shall be called, but few chosen" We know the analogy of the straight road, which leads to heaven. The other debatable point is that how does Holy Willie or indeed any of us know that we are going to heaven? The answer is that he doesn't know, but he assures himself that he will indeed be destined for heaven. This is similar to Hogg's "Confessions of a justified sinner" (see the next section).

Secondly, our future destination must enhance God's glory. Burns suggests that God is happy to consign people to hell, just for the sake of it. Is this the God, we know, the Father of Jesus? Or is it a perversion of Christianity as so many of the ideas that we humans have. But if you believe in Predestination i.e. that our destiny is forever fixed at birth this would seem to be a logical conclusion.

Thirdly, Burns may faithfully reflect eighteenth century theology but are his views true?

Firstly we do not know whether we are one of he elect or not. We may think we are, but what is the justification for this?

Secondly, Predestination leads to the idea that what we do doesn't matter if we are predestined for heaven or hell. If we are saved, we can do anything, either good or bad and we will land up in heaven anyway. But if we are going to hell, then we might as well do anything we like, because nothing will help us. Sometimes in the modern world this is called fate or "nothing that is for us will go past us". The idea that our destiny is fixed regardless is a very modern view, but it can lead to appalling crimes or a bleak indifference. You just need to hear of the words "Fate" or "Luck". Horoscopes also have the view that our destiny is fixed by our birthplace and the stars and planets. It is certainly not a Christian idea and a serious perversion of Christianity.

In Hogg's Confessions of a Justified Sinner we see a perverse example of this. A very good and serious young man is gradually convinced that he is one of the elect who is destined for heaven. Being one of the elect, he knows he is destined for heaven, regardless of what he does. He thereupon falls to various temptations and eventually even murders someone to prove he would do the ultimate evil deed and yet still have Salvation. He thought that nothing he did, could prevent him going to heaven. The hymn says " those who fain would serve Thee best are conscious most of wrong within" All of us are sinners and none can look confidently on the prospect of heaven except through the mercy of God and the sacrifice of Jesus.

And of course the answer to predestination is that one cannot know how he or she stands in the sight of God. Neither Holy Scripture nor the Church's tradition of faith asserts with certainty that any particular man or woman will eventually be in hell or will be saved and go to heaven. Hell is always held before our eyes as a real possibility, one connected to the offer of conversion and life. (The church's Confession of Faith, a Catholic Catechism for adults)

Another point about Burns' poem is that "no for any guid or ill they've dune afore Thee". The elect are not justified by their works, but by faith. And they are not saved by merit but by grace alone. While faith and faith alone saves, yet the Epistle of James says, "faith without works is dead" A proof of faith is what you are and what you do. The work we do is proof of our faith in Jesus.

Most of us would think that predestination is a perversion of the gospel. And we would be right about this. God has predestined no one to hell. And to support this argument we find a text in Paul's letter to Timothy. [132] "God, our Saviour, desires everyone to be saved and to come to the knowledge of the truth… for Christ Jesus, Himself human gave Himself for a ransom for us all"

SOME OTHER THINGS ABOUT HELL

Where is Hell in relation to our world?

Can we physically locate hell anywhere in the Universe or even out of it? The medieval picture of hell has gone forever. The ancients believed that hell was located in caverns under the earth and so Dante wrote this in his picture of hell. But this is no longer a reasonable opinion. Hell is not located in the physical world. Our resurrected bodies may be there but where is it? The Universe has many dimensions, not just length, breadth and height or even time. It is quite possible to locate both heaven and hell as co-dimensional with our universe or completely in another sphere of existence. These places would be something other than material existence, as we know it.

Prayer for the dead

Prayer on behalf of dead people has been a feature of Roman Catholic theology. This belief was rejected by the Reformers because of the abuse of these prayers by the Pre -Reformation Roman Catholic Church for financial reasons. But these prayers are mentioned here because of the belief that persons, who are in hell, can be transferred to heaven due to prayers on their behalf. Because of the problem of the correspondence of our time and eternal time are not the same, prayers for the dead made after death, were considered to be before death and could save a soul from hell after the time of death.

Stories about people who were saved through intercessions for them after death are numerous. One concerns St. Gregory the Great, who heard about the good deed of the pagan Roman Emperor, Trajan, towards a woman, whose son had been killed. Gregory prayed for the emperor, so that Trajan was admitted to heaven. Another story concerns St. Thecla, who prayed for a pagan woman Falconilla. A modern miraculous story is told of Don Bosco, who saved a fifteen year old boy from hell, by reviving him two days

---

[132] Timothy 3:4-6.

after he died and was asked if he wanted to live or go to heaven. The boy wanted to go to heaven.

This is the thought of the Roman Catholic Church, but it is not part of the beliefs of the reformed churches. However we cannot put any human limit on what prayers to God can do.

What about those who have never heard the Gospel?

The part we have just considered concerns those who have rejected the Gospel Those people are present day Marxists (a dwindling band today), Humanists and Materialists. But we have also to consider those who have never heard the gospel in this pluralist world. They comprise some believers in God such as Jews, Muslims, some kinds of Hindus and some others. They also comprise some other religions like Buddhists.

The problem is not new, Early in the Church's existence, there were debates about the Old Testament heroes. These men were much admired by the early Church. But as the saving work of Jesus is for all believers in God, then we may consider that other religious believers in God may be saved too.

There are some texts in the Bible, which teach that adherents of other religions can sometimes speak the truth about God. One such instance is that Paul cited Aratus while speaking to the Greeks in Athens. Paul said to the Athenians " What, therefore you worship as unknown, this I proclaim to you. " [133] Although we may declare that without Christ there is no salvation and that there is exclusiveness of salvation, we have these instances of people being saved apart from the knowledge of Christ. We cannot put any limits on how the Holy Spirit works.

The Devil and Hell

In the popular mythology of the 21st century, we have a picture of Satan or the Devil (who has alternative names like Auld Nick), who is supposed to live in hell. He is pictured as a half-human half-beast with horns and a tail and is usually pictured toasting unfortunate humans in an enormous fire. Is this a true account of the Devil? The main Christian view is that the Devil is a fallen angel and is the source of human evil. An alternative view is that evil is inside ourselves or coming from ourselves. The Devil is just an alternative way of expressing this view of evil.

In the New Testament many of the references of the Devil are allied to temptation. There is a text In Matthew, where Jesus says

---

[133] Acts 17:23.

to Peter "Get you behind me Satan. "[134] Jesus was tempted by the devil.[135] In Luke, there is the text "Then entered Satan into Judas, called Iscariot".[136] Again in Luke, we read that Jesus said "Simon, Simon, listen! Satan has demanded to sift all of you like wheat."[137] There are also general texts, linking Satan to sin. In Matthew, we read "If Satan casts out Satan"[138] In Luke, there is written "a daughter of Abraham, whom Satan has bound for eighteen long years"[139] In John, " you are from your father, the Devil and you choose to do your father's desires."[140]

Other texts are listed as follows: Paul said "And we do this, so that we may not be outwitted by Satan."[141] Paul also wrote, "a message of Satan is to torment me".[142] Peter wrote, "Your adversary, the devil, prowls around."[143] John wrote, "The children of God and the children of the devil are revealed in this way."[144] John also wrote, "the Son of God was revealed for this purpose, to destroy the works of the devil".[145]

In Revelation, John wrote "Where Satan's throne is"[146] and he also wrote, "there is a war in heaven", where the serpent is called a devil[147] and Satan was thrown down and the devil was bound for one thousand years."[148]

All the texts show that there is a force of evil called Satan or the Devil and he (Satan is always he) will eventually be destroyed.

It is up to you, the Reader, to consider the two accounts of evil.

Summary of the doctrine of Hell

We rely on pictures of hell. Some of these pictures come from the Bible and some from our own experience in this world. But we

---

[134] Matthew 16:23
[135] Matthew 4:1-11.
[136] Luke 22:31
[137] Luke 22:31
[138] Matthew 12:22
[139] Luke 13:16
[140] John 7:43-47
[141] 2 Corinthians 2:11
[142] 2 Corinthians 12:7
[143] 1 Peter 5:8
[144] 1 John 3:10
[145] 1 John 3:5
[146] Revelation 2:13
[147] Revelation 12:7-12:17
[148] Revelation 20

have to be cautious. We cannot say that we know nothing about hell, but on the other hand, we must be very cautious of giving detailed pictures of the geography of hell or who in this life are going there after their death. We can only rely on what pictures are given in the Bible and we must never make these pictures too concrete.

Hell is the great unknown of Christian theology today. It is commonly used in speech e.g. "Go to Hell" but the idea is not found in the services or sermons in church today. Over the last hundred years, any thought of hell has really disappeared from the church. So, some redemption of the doctrine of hell is necessary.

The main obstacle to the doctrine of hell is the thought of unending torture, but this is not a Biblical doctrine. A careful examination of the Bible passages about future punishment does not confirm the traditional view of hell as a place of torture. That view, where a person is resurrected to lasting torture in order to pay for their sins in this life, is only found in Judith in the Apocrypha and so is not a reliable source of evidence. The idea of torture owes its origin to the works of Augustine, which have been expanded by St. Thomas Aquinas.

If we decide that torture is not an integral part of hell then what is hell like? If it is the reverse of Heaven, it is the state of unending bleakness where joy and happiness are absent. Perhaps hell is more like a part of this present world, than the terrible pictures of someone's imagination.

Destruction is a common New Testament theme. What is meant by this idea? Is it just a warning about our present conduct? Perhaps when people are in hell, it means that they are but a shadow of their former selves.

One hopeful feature (and we must always have hope) is the picture of fire. Fire is not just the symbol of destruction, but it is also a symbol of purification. Metals are also made molten by fire and the impurities are then taken out, leaving the pure metal. The doctrine of purgatory was formulated for the purification of the sinners entombed there. If we reject the doctrine of purgatory, hell may have this purpose of purifying at least some humans, so that they will appear in heaven eventually.

We must also consider the possibility that eventually all may come to heaven. Some Bible texts would support this possibility. We must particularly remember that hell is a secondary item and not the main theme of the Bible, as might have been taught at one time. The Good News is resurrection after death with a new body for believers in heaven.

Karl Rahner said " We have to preserve alongside one another, without balancing them up, the principle of the power of God's general will for salvation, the redemption of all men through Christ, the duty to hope for the salvation of all men and the principle of the real possibility of becoming eternally lost."

At the end, we do not know how to reconcile the perfection of divine mercy, the bliss of the redeemed and the torment of the lost.

Chapter 9

COMMUNION of SAINTS

"We are surrounded by so great a cloud of Witnesses." [149]

We are interested in the destiny of ourselves and also the destiny of our family, our other relatives and our friends. It was so in New Testament times too, as we see in the letter of Paul to the Thessalonians.

All Saints Sunday is the first Sunday in November and is the Sunday where we commemorate the Communion of Saints. All Saints day (often a weekday) is one of the holiest days of the year (1 November) The reason why Halloween, the day previous to All Saints day, is the day where ghosts and witches supposedly roam around, is simply because it is the day before the holy day. Halloween was often an excuse for parties and still is. At one time in rural Scotland, Halloween was the time for a party for some good cause. There was among other things "dooking" for apples in tin tubs (not using your hands and the tubs were filled with water) and eating treacle scones with hands behind backs. But these events really had nothing to do with Halloween, but are a reminder that some events become fun days and are not really as serious as some Christians believe.

But why is the All Saints day particularly holy? Because the day is set aside to remember the truth about the influence of the saints who are all around us every day, but we remember them especially on that particular day.

A story from Italy:

Savonarola was a Dominican priest. He was a reformer, who lived in Florence. He was opposed to the very corrupt pope Alexander V1 (one of the Borgia family). He also helped the Democratic Government of Florence. However this upset the nobility, who wanted power. The result was that both parties, the Roman Catholic Church and the Government of Florence, wanted rid of him. Because of this, he was condemned to death as a heretic, a good excuse that had nothing to do with religion. When he was being burned a priest excommunicated him saying, "I separate you from the Church Militant and the Church Triumphant". Savonarola replied. "You can separate me from the Church Militant,

---

[149] Hebrews 12:1.

but you cannot separate me from the Church Triumphant for that is beyond your power.

What did Savonarola mean by the Church Triumphant? The Church Triumphant is the church of those who are now in heaven. The Communion of Saints is the church both the Church on earth (be it few in numbers or many persons) and the Church in heaven. Oddly the Communion of Saints has never been a popular doctrine. It is found in both main creeds, the Apostles Creed and the Nicene Creed, but when the Church of Scotland made an almost forgotten attempt to revise the Apostles Creed in 1992, it omitted this doctrine.

The Communion of Saints is the relationship of Christians to each other and also to the members of the Church, who are now in heaven. In former times a lady had her address book. Where a person died she wrote beside the name "Gone to Glory". Often we see in the "In Memoriam" services "safe in the arms of Jesus". The members of the Church who have died are still with us, as fellow members of the church of Jesus. We cannot see them, but they are there with Jesus in heaven. They do not need our prayers, although we can pray for them, but they can comfort us, not just by the knowledge that they are in heaven, but also by continually praying and interceding for us.

The saints in the Communion of Saints are not just those with the preface Saint. They are the whole of the Church in earth and now in heaven. They do not have nor need these extra heroic qualities of the Catholic Saints like St. Peter or St. Bernadette had, but are heroic in their own ways, trying to live and follow Jesus in their own time. They have not spent all their lives in worship or prayer, but have attended to all our needs each in their own way. We have lost many of the church members, who once worshipped with us, but they are only lost to us, but still remain members of the church and now worship God in heaven.

The Saints of the Catholic Church are also there in heaven. They were and are special people, not only because of their lives, but also because of their intercessions for us. We can pray to them if we wish, to Mary the mother of Jesus, to St. Bernadette, to St. Joan of Arc, to St. Francis of Assisi and to the others. But, as Protestants, we do not need to pray to them. We can go directly to Jesus in our prayers when we give thanks or need help.

Conclusion
　　The main point in the Communion of Saints is that prayer to God is not a lonely activity. We are sometimes on our own here on Earth and praying to God. But at the same time we are also praying along with others who are now dead, but with whom we are still in fellowship. It is not only the believers on earth we are in fellowship with, but also those who are now in heaven. The Communion of Saints is a fellowship of living and dead Christians in prayer to God.

Chapter 10

THE JUDGEMENT of THE DEAD

Sir Walter Scott, in his poem the Lay of the Last Minstrel, has a translation of the ancient poem Dies Irae. It says
"The day of Wrath, that dreadful day,
When Heaven and earth shall pass away",
"And you have come to Mount Zion and to the city of the living God, the heavenly Jerusalem and to innumerable angels in festive gathering and to the assembly of the first born who are enrolled in heaven. " [150]
"For all of us must appear before the judgement seat of Christ, that each may receive recompense for what has been done in the body, good or bad." [151]

Ancient Times and Judgement

The idea of judgement is not unique to Christianity. There is other ancient evidence of the belief that judgement comes immediately at death. People believed in individual judgement in ancient Egypt. This individual judgement also came immediately after death. The ancient Greeks also believed in an individual divine judgement.

Biblical
Old Testament Views on Divine Judgement

As we have seen above, the belief in judgement of the dead as well as God's judgement on the living did not first appear with Christianity but is also found in the prophetic books of the Old Testament and in Jewish works of the same period.
In the Old Testament, judgement consists of two different ideas.
The first idea, which is found in Isaiah, is the final judgement at the end of time called the Day of God. This final judgement is also found in Amos, who also mentions the day of the Lord. This is a day, coming at some time in the future where perfect judgement will be given and any wrongs righted.
The second idea is the present judgement, because of sin.
The present judgement has three elements.

---
[150] Hebrews 12:22
[151] 2 Corinthians 5:10

The first element is that the accuser in the judgement is God.
The second element in the judgement is condemnation by God.
The third element is the sentence of the judgement, which is pronounced by God and which is worked out in history.

In the Old Testament, judgement is mainly on nations, rather than on individuals. This is not exclusive to nations, as we find individual judgements given. An example of this is the condemnation of the false prophets, Ahab, son of Kolaiah and Zedekiah son of Manasseh for giving false prophecies on the future of the Kingdom of Judah. [152]

The New Testament and judgement

In the New Testament, the ideas of judgement are judgements on individual persons, rather than upon nations as in the Old Testament. There is a text "every knee will bow before Jesus." [153] Judgement is not just a future event, but there is also a present aspect to judgement. Because God is active in the present, the moral outcomes of our actions are important and are certainly not trivial. Judgement is not a threat, but is the means of making human beings examine their actions and repent of their wrong doings. The message of Jesus, however is not judgement but the message is salvation. "I came not to judge the world, but to save the world." [154] But the message of salvation makes judgement inevitable. The offer of salvation separates those who accept the offer and those who refuse the offer of salvation. The fact that some of the people who hear the message of salvation will refuse the offer makes judgement on them inevitable.

Christ's coming denoted victory over all the forces of evil. John wrote: "Now is the judgement of this world: now the ruler of this world (Satan) will be driven out." [155] Also on judgement John said, "because the ruler of this world (Satan) has been condemned." [156] Judgement is an incentive to self –examination and right living. Paul said, "If we judged ourselves we would not be judged." [157] Troubles and difficulties are a part of Judgement. Paul said, "this is evidence of the righteous judgement of God." [158] John wrote in

---

[152] Jeremiah 29 21-23
[153] Philippians 2:9
[154] John 12:47
[155] John 12:31
[156] John 16:11
[157] 1 Corinthians 11:31
[158] 2 Thessalonians 1:5

Revelation, "These are they, who came out of the great ordeal".[159] Another text from Revelation is "The souls of those who had been slaughtered for the word of God and for the testimony they had given."[160]

Names of the Day of Judgement

The names for the day of Judgement in the New Testament are as follows:
The day of the Lord,[161] The day of God,[162] The day of God's wrath,[163] The last day,[164] The day of Christ,[165] The day of the Lord Jesus,[166] The great day,[167] The day of redemption,[168] The day of vocation or the day Christ visits us,[169] The day of Judgement,[170] Eternal judgement,[171]

The church fathers and judgement

Judgement is found in the writings of the very early fathers of the Church, Barnabas, Second Clement and Polycarp. Clement stated that judgement would be just after death. Some theologians, Tertullian and Lactantius deny that there is a judgement at death, but instead all humans are detained awaiting the Last Judgement. Ambrose postulated that there would be storehouses where the souls would await judgement. In this period, the souls would be experiencing a foretaste of their ultimate destiny and would have some awareness of either blessedness or condemnation.
Jerome said there would be judgement on the day of death. Augustine wrote that there was an intermediate period between death and judgement. At the time of death, the soul would enter into torture or repose.

---

[159] Revelation 7:14
[160] Revelation 6:9
[161] 2 Peter 3:10 and 1 Thessalonians 5:2
[162] 2 Peter 3:12
[163] Romans 2:5
[164] John 3:6
[165] Philippians 2:16
[166] 1 Corinthians 5:5
[167] Jude 6
[168] Ephesians 4:30
[169] 1 Peter 2:12
[170] 1 John 4:17
[171] Hebrews 6:2

The Last Judgement in the Creeds (Apostles Creed, Nicene Creed and Athanasian Creed)

After the Second Coming it was believed that the dead would be judged and separated into those who would receive everlasting life and those who would be condemned. Judgement is a cosmic event and in the present ambiguous state of the world, good and evil are equally matched. Thus the Last Judgement is a kind of sifting where the distortions of evil will be finally defeated.

There have been problems in equating the ideas of a Saviour God in Pauline theology with the Jewish eschatology of the Last Judgement. This can be seen in the two creeds- the Nicene and the Athanasian.

The Nicene Creed declares "I believe...In our Lord Jesus Christ ...Who for us men and our salvation came down from heaven. And was crucified for us under Pontius Pilate. The third day He rose again according to the scriptures, and ascended into heaven and sitteth at the right Hand of the Father. And He shall come again with glory to judge both the quick (living) and the dead."

The so called "Athanasian Creed" or more correctly, "Quicunque Vult" "Christ suffered for our salvation: descended into hell, rose again on the third day from the dead. He ascended into heaven; He sitteth on the right hand of the Father, God Almighty, from whence He shall come to judge the quick and the dead. At whose coming all men shall rise again with their bodies: and shall give account for their own works. And they that have done well shall go into life everlasting. And they that have done evil into everlasting fire."
A similar version is given in the Apostles Creed.

Last Judgement and Mediaeval Christianity

Aquinas put together two apparently different judgements. He first considered if there would be a general judgement. Each human is both an individual person and is at the same time, a member of the human race. Therefore two fold judgements were due to him or her. One of the judgements is the particular judgement to which he or she would be subjected after death, when he or she would receive judgement according to their deeds, which they had done when they were alive. This would not happen entirely, but only partly, since they would not receive their judgement in the body, but only in the soul. The other judgement will be passed on him or her, as a member of the human race.

The sentence proper to this general judgement is the general separation of the good from the wicked, which would not precede this judgement. Yet, as regards the sentence on each individual, the judgement takes full effect immediately, since even the good individuals would receive an increase in reward after the judgement, both from the added glory of the body and from the completion of the number of the saints. Aquinas answered the question as to whether human beings would know their fates before the Last Judgement. The general judgement will be known more directly, than the judgement of each individual. Before the Last Judgement, each one will be certain of his own fate, but would not know the fate of everyone else. In this way, Aquinas explains the need for the Last Judgement. The thought of Aquinas on the Last Judgement is very difficult to understand.

Dante, in his Inferno, Circle 3 94-99, also wrote a passage about the Last Judgement.
"Thus spake my guide, "He'll rouse on more" he said,
Till the last loud angelic trumpet's sounding,
For when the Enemy Power shall come arrayed,
Each soul shall seek its own grave's mournful mounding,
Put on once more its earthly flesh and feature,
And hear the Doom eternally redounding "

The two great Judgements are:
Judgement of the nations.
Judgement of individuals.
The Judgement of the nations

As we have seen, one of the messages of the Old Testament is that nations too would be judged. This is worked out in history, when some of the immoral nations had been condemned to oblivion and other empires, which existed at the present, would also be condemned to oblivion. This happened in Old Testament times, when empires such as the Egyptian, the Babylonian and the Persian disappeared. But empires have disappeared since then. The Athenian Empire did not last long. The Roman Empire disintegrated and we have seen the German Empire of the Nazis, which was to last for one thousand years existed only thirteen years. The mighty Communist Empire all but disappeared within seventy years. God still judges nations today.

This is the message of a strange passage in Matthew, [172] which stated that all the nations would be gathered before Him.

---

[172] Matthew 25:31 to 48

Individual judgement sometimes called particular judgement

Blaise Pascal (1623-1662) was a French mathematician. He said "I know, O Lord, that at the instance of my death, I shall find myself entirely separated from the world, stripped naked of all things, standing alone before Thee, to answer to Thy justice, concerning all the motions of my thought and spirit." The thought of Pascal that there is an individual judgement at death is an orthodox Christian idea.

Judgement does not necessarily indicate that these events would all happen in one day in a single event as shown by artists, but that a judgement for all of us as individuals will certainly happen one day.

Who is the Judge of us all?

The answer is God. In one of the hymns by Henry Scott Holland, we read the following:
"Judge eternal Throned in Splendour,
King of Kings and Lord of Lords"
Jesus will make judgement. God gave the responsibility for judgement to Jesus. The Jewish leaders, by rejecting Jesus, brought judgement on themselves. Those who saw Christ's works have no excuse.
Jesus said: "I came into the world for judgement so that those who do not see, may see and those who see may become blind." [173]
"I do not seek my own glory, there is one who seeks it and He is the judge." [174]

Who will be judged?

Everyone will be judged. This can be seen in two parables of Jesus. Firstly the parable of the sheep and of the goats mentions judgement, [175] and secondly, the similar parable of the wheat and the tares (weeds) also implies judgement. [176]

These parables would indicate that some form of separation of the good and the bad would happen. These parables also teach that there will be rewards in heaven, for those who do good and misery in hell for those who do evil deeds.

---

[173] John 9:39
[174] John 8:50
[175] Matthew 25:31-34
[176] Matthew 13:30 and 13:41-43

Paul said "There will be anguish and distress for everyone who works evil." [177] Religious people will be judged as well as the most abominable sinners. In fact, judgement begins with religious people as most is expected of them. There are two texts concerning religious people: "Judgement will begin with the household of God." [178] "We, who teach, will be judged with greater strictness." [179]

Does what we did on earth matter when we are being judged?

Judgement is according to our works. Jesus said " As you did it to one of the least of these, who are members of my family, you did it to me." [180] "If you invoke the Father, the one who judges all people impartially according to their works live in reverent fear during your exile." [181]

Another passage about the consequences of our life in this world is the parable of the rich man and Lazarus. The reversal of the fortunes of the rich man and Lazarus the beggar clearly meant that their fates were decided immediately after death. "The poor man died and was carried by the angels to Abraham's bosom." The rich man's fate " The rich man died and was buried and in Hades, being in torment." The following passage is relevant. "Son, remember that you in your lifetime received your good things and Lazarus in like manner evil things; but now he is comforted here, and you are in anguish. And besides all this, between us and you a great chasm has been fixed, in order that those who passed from here to you may not be able, and none may cross from there to us." [182]

When will we be judged?

Judgement is immediate after death. The immediacy of the prospect of heaven and presumably judgement after death is found in statements of Jesus: Jesus said to the dying thief "Today, you will be with me in Paradise." [183] This means that judgement had already taken place and the dying thief was destined for heaven.

---

[177] Romans 2:9
[178] 1 Peter 4:17
[179] James 3:1
[180] Matthew 25:40 and Matthew 41:5
[181] 1 Peter 1:17
[182] Luke 16 25-26
[183] Luke 23:43

Jesus said "Those who believe in Him are not condemned, but those who do not believe are condemned already." [184] Jesus said "Anyone who hears my word and believes in Him, who sent me, has eternal life and does not come under judgement, but passes from death to life." [185]

Paul said in two texts that he visualised an immediate presence with Jesus after death. This means that judgement must have taken place at death. " I desire to die and be with Christ". [186] "We would rather be away from the body and at home with the Lord" [187]

To summarise, there is the problem as to whether judgement is immediately after death or as a cosmic event at the end of the universe. However this difference may be more apparent than real. It depends on the idea of time, where the time in this world goes on, but for those in heaven, the end of the world may be immediate as the future life is beyond time. However, for us here, we will learn immediately after death whether we are in heaven or not. The Great Assize, which is the name for everyone being judged together at the end of the universe, is just a pictorial way of saying this truth.

How can I be sure that whatever judgement is given that it will be just?

The main reason that you can trust the absolute justice of God, unlike the unfairness of this world is as follows:
God is just. So God's judgement is also just. It follows that the universe is a moral one. Sin is the enemy of God.

Judgement is serious, because sin is serious. God does take action in opposition to evil. The morality of the universe makes every deed and every action, which we have done throughout our lives, of the utmost importance. But it is this morality, which makes life worth living. Goodness has its own reward and so evil will also be rewarded.

Jesus told the parable of the wheat and the chaff " the chaff, He will burn with unquenchable fire." [188] Jesus said "As I hear, I judge: and my judgement is just because I seek not my own, but the will of Him who sent me". [189]

---

[184] John 3:18 and 19
[185] John 5:24
[186] Philippians 1:23
[187] 2 Corinthians 5:8
[188] Matthew 3:11
[189] John 5:30

Two other texts are: "The righteous judgement of God" [190] and also "The one who judges justly". [191]

What about mercy?
Perfect justice is mingled with mercy. "Paul said, "I received mercy because I acted ignorantly in unbelief and the grace of our Lord overflowed for me". [192] John Newton, in one of the hymns states:" I may my great accuser face, And tell Him, Thou hast died." We can escape the consequences of our works by believing that Jesus forgives sinners. We can rely on the mercy of God because His Son, Jesus died for us. This was the great act of God's mercy.

Can we condemn other people?
You must not condemn other people.
"Do not pass judgement on others." [193]
"You have no excuse whoever you are when you judge others for in passing judgement on another, you condemn yourself, because you, the judge, are doing the very same things. " [194] "

It is very important that we do not say, "He or She will be in hell" even if it refers to a person who is perceived to be extremely bad. We must leave final condemnation to God and not condemn others ourselves. This does not mean that the rule of law does not have a part to play in our present existence, as it is vital that we pass sentence on evil persons, especially for the safety of others, but in so doing we must not seek eternal condemnation.

THE GOOD NEWS
Christians will be assured that Judgement means that they will be assured of eternal life with Jesus. Christians should not fear Hell or even Judgement. That is the **GOOD NEWS.**

Paul said "For I know the one in whom I have put my trust and I am sure He is able to guard until that day, what I have entrusted to Him." [195]
"There is therefore no condemnation for those, who are in Christ Jesus." [196]

---

[190] 2 Thessalonians 1:6-10
[191] 1 Peter 2:23
[192] 1 Timothy 1:13
[193] Romans 2:6
[194] Romans 2:1
[195] 2 Timothy 1:12
[196] Romans 8:1

The Great Assize

What do we make of the idea of the Great Assize where all the dead people of every age (billions of them) will be assembled at one great gathering and be judged? From this assize, they will be vindicated or condemned to go either to heaven or hell. The idea of the Great Assize is found in 2 Esdras[197] and is repeated in Revelation. [198] In Revelation 20, the judge is seated on a great white throne. Everyone is judged according to his or her works. The books, including the Book of life, were opened. Anyone whose name was not found in the book of Life was thrown into a lake of fire.

However, what is the point of assembling everyone for the people to be to be ordered to go back to heaven or to hell? Also the New Testament basis for this Great Assize, (which as you will see later in art) is rather doubtful. The only text for this is a single passage in Revelation, which is not necessarily to be taken literally. St. John in Revelation had a vision, which was a pictorial description of a real message. Both Augustine and Aquinas also thought that the passage was not to be taken literally, but allegorically. The point of the Great Assize is a valid and very moral one, in that we must all account for our lives. But it is just not permissible to make this picture of the Great Assize concrete and historical and so we would then have two judgements.

It is interesting that, in order to save the Great Assize as a historical event, one modern writer, Jim Graham, denies judgement at death. This writer, in order to save the idea of the Great Assize equates Paradise with Hades. Surely, this is not a valid option. If we reach Paradise, surely this is another name for heaven?

The morality of judgement

The judges in the courts today, weigh up the evidence, find the accused guilty or not guilty, and finally pass sentence. But the judges in New Testament times were not like that. These judges, as kings or householders also gave out rewards. Our reward for believing in Jesus is eternal life with Him in heaven.
There is here an apparent tension, which is more apparent than real, between the roles of Jesus as a Saviour and as a Judge of mankind. The ideas have been placed side by side in Christian theology. Jesus is both Saviour and Judge.

---

[197] 2 Esdras 7
[198] Revelation 20

Jesus as Saviour

The idea of Jesus as Saviour can be traced back to Paul, and is his response to the difficulty of the Jewish idea of judgement, which did not appeal to the Gentiles. Paul saw the death of Jesus as a divinely planned event. God had to rescue human beings from sin, both the original sin and our own sins. Original sin seems an unpleasant doctrine, but we soon see that even if we do not sin, as a baby is not usually capable of realising sin, nonetheless we have a potentiality for sin, which will sooner or later express itself. There is also the continued sinning of all of us. Paul had the conception of Jesus as a Saviour God who came to rescue the world from sin. Paul thought that good works was not enough to save us. "Since all have sinned and fall short of the glory of God, they are now justified by His grace as a gift, through the redemption that is in Christ Jesus whom God put forward as a sacrifice of atonement by his blood." [199]

Jesus as Judge.

The idea of Christ as judge comes from Jewish thought. It can be seen in the passage in Mark with Jesus saying "The time is fulfilled, and the kingdom of God has come near, repent and believe in the good news." [200] This is a prophetic situation, which implies an end of the present world order and the divine vindication of Israel. It is a Jewish national event when the Jews will be vindicated and implies a resurrection of the dead. The Jewish disciples and the early Jewish Christian Church associated Jesus with this end of time event. The disciples asked the risen Jesus "Lord is this the time when you will restore the kingdom to Israel?" [201]

Self-knowledge.

God's judgement to human beings is about giving humans His self-knowledge (Brunner). Death is a moment of truth. Judgement is not a once for all verdict of blessedness or condemnation, but is a gradual process of self-knowledge. In Judgement, humans must make a choice. God is involved in this choice. He desires that man must choose the way of life and He must press His case. Judgement is part of this life. But judgement is much more devastating after death.

---

[199] Romans 3:24 and 25
[200] Mark 1:15
[201] Acts 1:6

The Last judgement and art.

The Last Judgement and the Great Assize are the subjects of many paintings. These were popular subjects, even more than heaven or hell. There are also several artistic works, which are not part of the judgement at death but rather paintings of the Great Assize. The subject of the Last Judgement lends itself to imaginative paintings, especially of the damned.

Summarising the Last Judgement.

There are six principle thoughts on the last judgement.

Firstly Judgement is both a present and a future activity. We are judged now as well as in the future.

Secondly, The idea of the Last Judgement is to confirm the state and reward of the righteous people. Those already in heaven will only have their judgement confirmed in their new life in heaven. The Christian believer will have mercy and so will assuredly have the prospect of heaven.

Thirdly, in the Last Judgement, the purposes of God in our earthly lives will be made manifest both to our neighbours and to us. At the Last Judgement, the meaning of God's will for us and for the world will be disclosed.

Fourthly, For the people who have never heard the gospel and who have remained faithful to other religions, they will also have the prospect of heaven. We may be sharing heaven with Jews and Muslims.

Fifthly for the modern materialists, who have heard the gospel and rejected it, there will be no future. Whether hell or total destruction, their judgement will be condemnation.

Sixthly, for Christian believers, there is the prospect of mercy as well as judgement. The future of Christians is a life with God and Jesus in heaven. Jesus said, "I am come not to judge the world but to save the world." [202]

---

[202] John 12:47

Chapter 11

THE SECOND COMING OF JESUS

"Lo! He comes with clouds descending,
Once for favoured sinners slain,
Thousand thousand saints attending,
Swell the triumph of His reign,
Alleluia! Alleluia! Alleluia!
God appears on earth to reign." [203]

The Second Coming of Jesus is the term, which the church has given, to the belief that Jesus will come again to earth. It is sometimes called the Parousia. The early Christians believed that this coming would happen in their own time and that Jesus would come again in bodily form. Today, the belief is that Jesus will come again at the end of time (or the end of the world or universe). Then Jesus would be associated with an event, which did not belong to the present age. If we accept this, Jesus would not return as long as the present universe lasts.

The Second Coming is the most difficult part of Christian belief. It is simple in that it is easily understandable, but it does not fit too well with our ideas of heaven and hell. There is today a reaction against the traditional views of heaven and hell, with a changed emphasis on the Second Coming with which some theologians want to replace the Christian hope of heaven. To do this, they ignore some of the New Testament texts about heaven and hell.

Biblical
Old Testament

The belief in the coming of the Kingdom of God was a long-standing Jewish belief. It was particularly prominent in the Jewish books of the first century BC and the first century AD. The Jews divided time into two ages the present age and the age to come. The age to come would be the age of God, when everything would be put right. This would happen after the Day of the Lord, a cosmic and earth shattering event when God would intervene. Thereafter the age of God would be inaugurated.

The idea of what the world would be like after the Messiah came is something similar to our idea of heaven. There would be peace, plentiful harvests and friendship of ourselves with the beasts and

---

[203] Charles Wesley

the friendship of the beasts with each other. This can be seen in some of the passages from Isaiah. "The wolf would live with the lamb." [204]

This belief in the Day of the Lord was associated with a heavenly figure called the Messiah. He would come as a leader, who would conquer the other nations and establish a Jewish kingdom like the kingdom established in the reign of David and Solomon. Thus the Messiah would be a powerful political figure. Some of the Jewish ideas were most unworthy. The Jews dreamed of conquest of the other nations. But some Jewish ideas were noble in that the Jews would bring other nations to the true worship of God. Isaiah said "I have given you as a covenant to the people, a light to the nations." [205] This new age would be the work of God directly, but would be inaugurated by this human figure, the Messiah. The day of the coming of the Messiah also involved judgement of all the nations.

New Testament

The Christian Church in the first century AD took the current Jewish beliefs and re-interpreted these beliefs. The Day of the Lord was interpreted by the early church as the day of the Second Coming of Jesus.

The New Testament, especially the Gospels, has a large number of texts, which are thought to refer to the Second Coming of Jesus. I shall go into these texts in detail and then try to give a coherent account of these. But it is evident that many of the texts do not refer to the Second Coming of Jesus, but to other events.

The four possibilities are:

1) Prophecies or forecasts from Jesus about His coming death and resurrection. This is clearly seen in many of His parables. John Robinson suggested that all the references in the Gospels about a future coming refer to His death and resurrection and the disciples misinterpreted the meaning. He may have overstated his case, but it is certain that many of the parables about watchfulness refer to the events of the death and resurrection of Jesus.

2) Prophecies of the fate of the Jews after the time of Jesus. This reference is to the Jewish revolt 66 AD-71 AD, which ended in the destruction of Jerusalem and the temple. This is pretty clear in the Mark, Luke and Matthew. [206] [207] [208] Jesus did feel for the Jewish

---

[204] Isaiah 11:6
[205] Isaiah 42:6
[206] Mark 13:14-37

people and He wept over the fate of Jerusalem. He saw all too clearly what would happen thirty years after His death. Mark's gospel was written about AD 60 with information probably collected by Mark from Peter's preaching over many years. The Jerusalem church would possibly have a copy of it and some of the members would have recollected the actual words of Jesus thirty years before. When the Jewish revolt happened, the church members would have decided that too many of the prophecies of Jesus were just about to happen and they left Jerusalem for Pella in the country that is now Jordan. The matter that interests us in this is that these prophesies did refer to an actual event that happened some thirty years after the crucifixion and not to the far distant future.

3) Prophecies about the end of the world or universe. These were inherited from Judaism. [209] The Jews believed that the world would end with a vindication of God's righteousness.

4) Despite the fact that some of the texts, which might be thought to refer to a Second Coming of Jesus, do not refer to that event, some other texts do refer to the Second Coming of Jesus. Some theologians have said that Jesus believed that He would return soon and Jesus was mistaken in His belief. But there is no evidence that He said He would soon return to the earth. The disciples frequently misunderstood what Jesus meant and if they thought that Jesus would soon return, this is not very surprising.

The date of the Second Coming is referred to in various ways
"The day of Christ Jesus" [210]
"The day of Christ" [211]
"His coming" [212]
"That day" [213]
"His appearing and His Kingdom." [214]

The New Testament refers to the Second Coming as an event and makes several statements about that event.

Firstly, it would be an open public event. It would not be a secret. "As the lightening comes from the East and flashes as far as the West, so will the Coming of the Son of Man." [215]

---

[207] Matthew 24:15-31
[208] Luke 21:20-26
[209] Matthew 25:31-46
[210] Philippians 1 verse 6
[211] Philippians 1 verse 10
[212] 1 John 2:28
[213] 2 Timothy 4:8
[214] 2 Timothy 4:1.

"The Lord Jesus is revealed from Heaven with his mighty angels in flaming fire". [216]

"The Son of Man is coming in a cloud with power and great glory." [217]

Secondly, the Coming would be associated with immediate and simultaneous judgement of the believers and the wicked.

"Inflicting vengeance on those who do not know God and on those who do not obey the gospel of our Lord Jesus." [218]

Thirdly, the Second Coming would be the ultimate end point of the hope for the future of the believers in Jesus.

"The Lord himself will descend from heaven. We will be with the Lord forever." [219]

"We wait for the revealing of our Lord Jesus Christ." [220]

Fourthly, the Second Coming is important, both for those who are now in heaven and also for those alive when Jesus comes again. The passage, which is quoted below must not be taken too literally, but it means that there will be a changed existence after the Second Coming, even for those in heaven now.

"The dead in Christ will rise first. Those, who are alive, who were left will be caught up in the clouds together with them to meet the Lord in the air." [221]

Fifthly, there is a promise of a new future after the Second Coming of Jesus.

"New heavens and a new earth where righteousness is at home." [222]

"The glory about to be revealed to us. " [223]

Timing of the Second Coming

There are several texts concerning the time of the Second Coming. The message is very clear in that we do not know the time of this event, whether next week or ten thousand years from now.

---

[215] Matthew 24:27 and Luke 17:24.
[216] 2 Thessalonians 1:6-10.
[217] Luke 21:27.
[218] 2 Thessalonians 1:8.
[219] 1 Thessalonians 4:16.
[220] 1 Corinthians 1:7.
[221] 1 Thessalonians 4: 16 and 17.
[222] Romans 8:18.
[223] 2 Peter 3:13.

"It is not for you to know the times or periods that the Father has set by his own authority." [224]
"You know not the day nor the hour." [225]
"About the date, no one knows only the Father." [226]
"The Son of Man is coming at an unexpected hour. " [227]

The Early Church and the timing of the Second Coming

As far as the time of the event (the Day of the Lord), the early Christians seemed to forget the words of Jesus that no one knows the time of the event and expected this event to come in their lifetime. As the years went on and more Christians died, they realised that the Day would not come in their lifetime. The Second Coming became a future event without a fixed time as Jesus had said.

Modern Ideas- The end of the world or universe.

Jesus himself said that we do not know the hour or the day when this coming will happen. However, many of His followers since His lifetime have stated that they do know when the end would happen. There was a belief that the end of the world would happen on a certain day (like 1000 AD). This belief that the end of the world would come on a certain day came from some abstruse calculation (usually based on some text in Revelation). This has been a constant belief of certain Christian or even non-Christian sects. But following the words of Jesus, this event could happen tomorrow or 100,00 years from now or any other date you think might be relevant.

Matthew has a text that the end will not come until the gospel is preached to all nations. This means that the end is a long way off. The idea of the Second Coming is important in that it guarantees that every event is not meaningless. Everything will be made right one day in the future. Our world has a meaning, and the meaning is that there will be a future life with Jesus.

Is the Kingdom of Heaven here now?

Here is the statement of Jesus in Luke that the Kingdom of God is here now i.e. that the life of Jesus inaugurates the Kingdom of God. This is called "realised eschatology". The paradox is that the Kingdom of Heaven is partly here now, because of the life and work

---

[224] Acts 1:7.
[225] Matthew 25:13.
[226] Mark 13:2
[227] Luke 12:39 and 40.

of Jesus, but also it is partly in the future. The kingdom of Heaven will not be fully accomplished until the end of the age, when Jesus will come again.

What is to happen?
The Bible reveals that Jesus will come again at the end of the world or possibly the Universe. And also that Jesus will inaugurate a new creation involving all the people alive at that time and dead Christians, who are heaven now and possibly some or all of the persons, who are now in hell.

The idea of the Second Coming of Jesus, which will happen someday and the knowledge that dead Christians are in heaven now, do not really conflict with each other. The dead Christians are in heaven now, as Jesus said. The Second Coming is at the end of the universe, as we know it. The end of the universe will happen, the Sun will grow cold or some cataclysmic event will happen on earth such as being hit by a large meteorite. This will not occur by human hands and not even by a human made atomic bomb or by biological warfare. It will happen because God wills it and not because of human wickedness and carelessness of the universe that humans have been entrusted with. A completely new universe not related to our present universe will be inaugurated and it will be something like heaven. The dead persons, who are in heaven now, will be a part of this new universe. And maybe even those in hell will be part of the new universe too.

The Second Coming and Art
The biblical end of the world is represented in an eighth century picture by Beatus called Martino and Petrus, clericus. This art was designed to illuminate a manuscript called Apocalypse, which gave the story of the end of the world. A modern painter, who described the events after the Second Coming of Jesus, was Stanley Spencer. Among the events he described in pictures was the preaching of Jesus at the regatta at Cookham and the post resurrection pictures of workers at Port Glasgow. He depicted the persons, whom he painted, who were on earth after the Second Coming as ordinary human beings and not angels with wings. He also painted "The hill of Zion.

The Second Coming and hymns.
The Second Coming has been the theme of a number of hymns especially "Lo, He comes with clouds descending" (the first verse is in the title to the chapter) "At the name of Jesus", "Come thou long

expected Jesus, " "Thy Kingdom come on bended knee", Hail to the Lord's anointed" and "Mine eyes hath seen the glory". These are popular and frequently sung.

Millenarianism

The Millennium is derived from the word mille, meaning 1000. This signifies the thousand-year existence of an earthly kingdom, following the Second Coming of Jesus. And the result is the establishment of a totally new world order. As we have seen, Jesus said that no one knows the day or the hour when the kingdom will come.

Nevertheless there have been numerous attempts to do this throughout the ages. This was particularly important in that time of the Church Fathers, who believed this event, would happen in their own time. This was especially the belief of Irenaeus and Tertullian. There have also been other attempts to give various dates for this event. One favourite date was1000 AD. Other dates have been in favour, often based on weird and abstruse calculations.

But there have also been people, who believed that we are now at the end of time. One instance happened in second century Turkey, when two prophetesses stated that the Second Coming was imminent and that Jesus would come near to their villages, causing people to leave their homes. Another instance was after the Edict of Milan (313 AD), when Christians believe that the last days of the earth had come. The Roman Empire (after 313 AD) followed by the Holy Roman Empire was the 1000 year reign forecasted in the Bible.

Millenarianism is a belief that occurs every so often. There is no good evidence to suggest this is other than a mistaken belief, but it can have serious repercussions for the individuals concerned. Mediaeval theologians discussed how many angels could sit on the end of a pin. (The answer is none or billions) However this is only of interest to angels. Modern theologians have different views on the millennium. Dispensational Premillennialism, Classical Premillennialism, Postmillennialism, and Amillennialism have all been argued at length. These are really only of interest to academic theologians. If the reader is interested, the book "*The promise of the future*" by Cornelius Venema deals with this at length.

The theology of hope

Theology changed (not for the first time) after the carnage of the First World War. The current theological idea then was a liberal theology with ideas of human progress. Karl Barth was a German theologian who turned the theological world upside down. He said that we cannot reach God and that He must come down to us. The natural theology, such as was stated by St. Thomas Aquinas, expounded the idea that we could see God in the natural world, but Barth's theology had a far more transcendent view of God. Barth's ideas were valid for his time and still hold a fascination for us. Tillich and Bultmann modified Barth's ideas. These ideas were even more modified by John Robinson, whose "Honest to God" created a storm. American theologians Hamilton and Altizer took the ideas further stating the death of God. Theology had come to a dead end. However other German theologians, Pannenberg and Jurgen Moltmann took a different line. Moltmann concentrated on eschatology and in particular the end of the world. His focus was the coming of God and the renewal of all creation. The idea of the Second Coming goes back to the New Testament. Jesus said to his disciples that He would come again and take them to Himself. In the early Church this would give hope for the future and Moltmann thought that at the present time the renewal of all creation would provide hope for the future.

Secular future hope has gone with the complete collapse of Communism and with it Marxist ideology where the Communists gave a supposed hope of an ideal world in the future. The promised Marxist utopia did not become a utopia, but a nightmare with riches for the few leaders and virtual slavery for the rest. The technological world is also supposed to be heaven on earth, but is proving to be much different from heaven on earth.

The Coming of God presents a Christian hope for the future. But this also has some difficulties. The return of Jesus was to signal a new heaven and a new earth and this would involve all creation, both the living and the dead humans and all plants and animals too. Thus heaven and hell are replaced by a new creation of the universe.

Problems of the Second Coming

There are various problems about the Second Coming, problems, which have not been fully explained:

1- The timescale. The entry to this new creation is not immediate but could be 500,000 years from now. Jesus said that no one knows the day or the hour but the hope is less if the future is so distant that it may be out of sight.

2- The problem of where the dead people are now. In the early church, it was proposed that there would be storehouses for the dead awaiting the final resurrection. Today the belief is that the dead are in heaven now, as Jesus said, and the dead would have resurrected bodies which are different from our present material bodies.

3– The idea of the renewal of all creation of the entire universe is possible, as God can do anything. Has the thought of renewal been thought through, knowing that there is a very vast universe? If the idea of heaven in another sphere of existence is perfectly conceivable, then it must be incorporated into ideas about the Second Coming of Jesus.

4– It is difficult to completely tie in the Second Coming with heaven and hell. This however is not impossible if heaven was somehow incorporated in the new universe at the end of time.

5-The idea that the future world will include all humanity rather negates the idea of judgement and the idea of justice. Some individuals set their face against Christianity and also against any idea of doing any good deeds in this world. The New Testament is very moral and has a very strong sense of justice. But there is a Biblically based belief in universal salvation, which would happen eventually. The case for universal salvation has been discussed fully.

6-There is some merit in the idea that any future must include the earth. But some of the theologians put far too much emphasis on the cosmic dimension rather than the fate of individuals. When you come to the cosmic idea, it is a far off event and it is all too easy to forget individual happiness. We must not fall into the trap of the Communists who put future welfare before the welfare of the individual.

Summary.

The Second Coming is well attested in the Bible and subsequent belief of the Christian Church. It is based on the belief that there is a moral universe and that all will be made right one day. It has unexplained problems, but that does not take away from the importance of the event even, if it may be rather distant.

Chapter 12

Conclusions of the book

'Tis mystery all! The Immortal dies
Who can explore his strange design?
In vain, the first born seraph tries,
To sound the depths of love divine" [228]

The main purpose of the book is to give some idea of the evidence for an afterlife and also some consideration as to what this afterlife might be like. This is both for contemporary Christians who may be confused as to what we could reasonably believe today and also for inquiring non-believers. This account of the hereafter has been written as an orthodox Christian account of belief, where the Bible is used as far as possible to confirm the beliefs. Some modern theologians have emphasised the Second Coming of Jesus and the renewal of all Creation; we must never ignore the hope of attaining heaven.

The soul or self or mind

A belief in the soul or mind or self is critical to having a belief in the hereafter. We are not just material beings, but we have an immortal soul, which transcends death. Our true person is immortal.

Our final destiny

Our destiny is to live with Jesus in heaven. Some atheists (e.g. Feuerbach) have described this as wishful thinking, because we want to believe in a life after death. Human beings have believed in a life after death from the earliest times. The reverse also applies. Disbelief in the hereafter may also be wishful thinking. We may want to believe in heaven, but the doctrine also applies to belief in hell and judgement and who desires these things? We cannot verify now that we will be in heaven one day. However, we will be able to verify the existence of heaven after our deaths when we arrive there. This is called eschatological verification. (McQuarrie) We must remember that faith, either in life after death or in no life after death is what we cannot prove. That is what faith is all about.

---

[228] Charles Wesley And can it be verse 2

Heaven

"Where is heaven?" says the young child. Heaven is really in two parts. On the one hand the kingdom of heaven is now, as Jesus has appeared into this world. On the other hand there is a future heaven after death. Perhaps, even the ancient world did not believe that heaven was somewhere in the sky, but was situated beyond everything that they knew. The possibility is that there could be room for another existence in another dimension. The dimensions we recognise are length, breadth and height and time is a possible fourth dimension. So heaven could well exist as another dimension or dimensions, so that our soul or self could well exist after death in another dimension or sphere.

What then could heaven be like?

A simple description that it is just Paradise or a beautiful place, where we will be close to God and Jesus. We can only talk of heaven by means of analogies to this world, as we know nothing else. There are many examples to choose from such as beauty. If we see beauty on earth, we shall see it in heaven. Heaven is perfect, so attributes like envy, jealousy, or ugliness have no place there. As all our physical attributes are left behind, we would need to have new bodies, which are usually called glorified bodies. This body will be material in some way and not akin to a dream world as some people have thought. The material, which makes up our heavenly body, will not be the same kind of substance as our present body. It is not easy to visualise of what quasi-material nature they could consist. But these bodies would need to be recognisable in order that we could be seen as separate persons who are still the persons we have known on earth. We will retain our individuality in heaven and it will not be a case of absorption in to God with the loss of our individuality, as many mystics have thought.

It is essential for a belief in heaven that we retain our memory of our life on earth. There must be some possible way in order that memory can de transferred from ourselves from the time we were living on earth to our future life in heaven. When we live here on earth, we are just energy and not composed of solid particles, as we seem to be. Is matter not just energy? It is not unlikely that some memory of what we are now can be transferred into another dimension. And if this can be done, the person in heaven can simply be a resurrected person with a new body with the appearance of the same body as we had on in earth. The appearance of this new body could be the same as what the person had at a suitable time in their life and not just the body the person had at death. All this presupposes that our real self is not our present material body and there is a dimension containing heaven and hell, which is connected in some way with our present dimension here on earth.

We can only ascend to heaven after death, by the work of Jesus and accepting the offer so freely made concerning the forgiveness of our sins. If we hate so much that we cannot accept the sacrifice of Jesus or are atheists, then we may be destroyed or live in hell for some time if not for all eternity. If we think (like Origen) that the Christian gospel means that many or all people will be saved eventually, some of us will be in hell for an indefinite period and then go to heaven. We shall then see Jesus in heaven.

Hell
Hell is the most controversial part of Christian belief. But the possibility of any person going to hell after death must remain in order to provide an incentive for morality in this life. Hell must remain a possibility, but we must not say about any person that he or she is so bad that the are going to hell after death. No individual was condemned to hell in the Gospels. On the other hand, the preaching in the Gospels is straightforward in that we must think of the possibility of hell for ourselves. Every person must continually put in front of them the possibility that they might be in hell after death.

What is Hell like?
Hell would seem to be a sort of dreich intermediate state between this present life and our eventual final fate. There is no justification for a belief in eternal torture as the only Biblical text for this is in Judith. But hell is not the same as heaven. While God is not completely absent from us there, we are not close to God there. Life in Hell will not be like the life of joy of heaven. The pictures of hell as fire are pictures designed to show hell as an undesirable place.

Is hell forever?
Hell is not eternal, as we are not necessarily there forever. In the Bible there are examples (e.g. Gehazi's leprosy), where the word "eternal" (in the Greek translation of the Old Testament) does not mean going on forever. The possibility of salvation is always there in the New Testament. It is also possible at some of those in hell may be given a second chance. Some may take this opportunity but it is possible that some may refuse it. Will God then say "Thy will be done"? The fate of those people in hell could be total destruction or

final extinction or some kind of complete emptiness or everlasting existence without God. Perhaps humans are so made that they will all repent and be reconciled to God at the end of time. It is wise not to be too dogmatic about their eventual fate. It cannot be stated too often that the New Testament is not about hell, but about the good news of Jesus and our salvation and our future in heaven. But hell is part of our belief and we cannot ignore it. Morris stated that "The kind hearted Victorians abolished Hell, but found that they did away with Heaven too".

Communion of Saints or the Church Triumphant

This belief can be described as the dead Christians, who are now in heaven, have a connection with us in that they are praying for us now and working for us in their own ways. It is also a comforting belief, that our life here is not the end of everything and that we have a future in front of us.

Judgement of the living and the dead

We are living under judgement even now. Judgement begins in our present life. Judgement is what happens to every one of us. But what is the result of judgement? Are we to face the Great Assize, which is described in the Book of Revelation? Based on the dying thief, who is now in Paradise, there is evidence that we go to heaven immediately after death. Also, the Roman Catholic Church has always believed that the Catholic saints went directly to heaven after death. So this makes this story of the Great Assize in Revelation, more of a vision or a dream of heaven than a concrete future reality. To make the idea of the Great Assize more intelligible, some theologians said that Paradise was not heaven and that it is the garden outside heaven. Thus our future in heaven is not assured at death.

In summing up, Judgement is really a confirmation of our eternal existence rather than the thought of a pass or fail exam. We must not confuse judgement with judges passing sentence in the law courts. Although God judges us, we really judge ourselves by our actions and lack of faith.

The Second Coming of Jesus

It is difficult to tie in the Second Coming with belief in heaven and hell. If we believe we have instant access to heaven after death, heaven seems a near and credible belief. The Second Coming at the end of the earth's existence may be far away. Of course, we cannot be sure how far away the end really is.

There is one other problem about the Second Coming. If we are in heaven at the time the return of Jesus to this Earth, where do we go then? How are heaven and this universe amalgamated into a new creation? Is there to be a renewal of the universe with the inhabitants of heaven or is there to be an amalgamation of Heaven and this universe?

A modern view of the hereafter might be as follows:
1) Temporal death
2) The particular or temporary judgement (immediately after death)
3) Eternal life in heaven or damnation in hell (temporarily or forever)
4) The Second Coming of Jesus at the end of the world or universe. This is both to wrap up worldly existence forever and to give entry to heaven or hell for those living at that future time.
5) The new existence.

No one has been able to work out the exact relationship between a life in heaven after death and a future universe after the Second Coming. What we have to do is to trust Jesus that He will look after us whatever the final outcome will be for us.

St Paul said "Eye has not seen, nor ear heard, neither have entered into the heart of man, the things that God has prepared for those who love Him."

Appendix 1

Texts on heaven, Hell, Judgement and the Second Coming of Jesus.

Texts on Heaven

Heaven and earth passing away in Matthew 5:18 and Luke 16:17
Our Father in heaven in Matthew 5:45 and 6:9 (The Lord's prayer) also Luke 11:2.
Heaven opened in Luke 3:21 and John 1:51.
Heaven shut up in Luke 4:25
Angels in heaven in Mark 13:32
Clouds of heaven in Mark 14:62
Lord of heaven and earth in Luke 10:21 and Acts 17:24.
Parable of the Prodigal son (sinned against heaven) in Luke 15:18.
Powers of heaven in Luke 21:25
Rooms in heaven in John 14:1.
Remain in heaven in Acts 3:21
Caught up into third heaven in 2 Corinthians 12:2-4.
Things in heaven in Ephesians 1:10 and Colossians 1:10.
Heavenly places in Ephesians 2:6.
Hope in heaven in Colossians 1:5
Citizenship of heaven in Philippians 3:20
Heavenly country Hebrews 11:13-16.
Swear by heaven in James 5:12.
Kept in heaven in 1 Peter 1:4
New heaven in 2 Peter 3:13 and Revelation 21 and 22.
Heaven opened in Revelation 19:11.
Jerusalem above in Galatians 4:26
Hope He has called you in Ephesians 1:18.
My desire is to depart and be with Christ in Philippians 1:23
Inheritance of the saints in the light in Colossians 1: 12:
Glorious inheritance among the saints in Ephesians 1:18.
God prepared beforehand to be a way of life in Ephesians 2:10.
The things that are above where Christ is seated in Colossians 3:1.
The city that is to come in Hebrews 13:14:
Paradise of God in Revelation 2:7,

Texts on Hell

Jesus mentions hell 15 times in the Gospels.
Whole body cast into hell Matthew 5:29, 5:30, Luke 12:5.
Hell of fire Matthew 5:22.
Destroy soul and body in hell Matthew 10:28, Luke 12:5.

Woe to Capernaum (Hades) Matthew 11:23, Luke 10:15.
Gates of hell (Hades) Matthew 16:18.
Two eyes cast into hell Matthew 18:9, Mark 9:47, Luke 18:9.
Child of hell Matthew 23:15
Sentenced to hell Matthew 23:33
Lifted up his eyes in torment (Rich man) Luke 16:23.
Other texts are as follows:
Warnings about a possible fate
Saying that you are a fool in Matthew 5:22 and Luke 12 57-59
Throwing out eyes and limbs which offend in Matthew 5:29 and 30 and18: 8 and 9, Mark 5:29-31, Mark 9:43 and 45 and 47.
Fire is never quenched in Mark 9:48.
Destroy body and soul in hell in Matthew 10:28.
Authority to cast into hell in Luke 12:5.
Eternal fire Matthew 25:41.
Furnace of fire Matthew 13:46 and 50
Rejection and Destruction
Into outer darkness Matthew 21:13 and 25:30
Parable of the narrow door in Luke 13:23-29.
Parable of the narrow gate in Matthew 7:13 and 14.
Parable of the ten girls at the wedding in Matthew 25:10-12.
Parable of the servant with one talent In Matthew 25:30.
Parable of the healing of the servant and debarring him from the kingdom in Matthew 8 10-12
Parable of the tares in Matthew 13:30 and 36-43.
Parable of the man at the wedding without wedding clothes in Matthew 22:14
Parable of the tree known by its fruit in Matthew 7:19
Parable of the fig tree in Luke 13:9.
Parable of the net and the rejected fish in Matthew 13:50.
King's response to the declining guests in Matthew 22:7
Wise and foolish builders in Matthew 7:27 and Luke 16:19
Woes: Capernaum Matthew 11:23. Chorazin Luke 10:13.
Bethaisda Matthew 11:22
Hypocrites in Matthew 7:22 and 23.
Repent or perish: in Luke 13:5
Flee from the wrath to come in Matthew 3 7-12.
Making life secure and losing it. In Matthew 10:39 and16: 25-27, Mark 6 35-37, Luke 9 24-25 and 17:33.
Retribution.
Parable of the rich man and Lazarus in Luke 16:19-31
Parable of the unfaithful servant in Matthew 24:45-51 and Luke 12:47.

Parable of the sheep and the goats in Matthew 25:46.
Sayings against the Pharisees and scribes
Matthew 23:15 and 33.
General mention of hell in the gospels
Not even the gates of hell in Matthew 16:18
Sin against the Holy Spirit in Matthew 12 31 and 32.
Offences against children (maybe the disciples) in Mark 9:42 and Matthew 18:6
Lift up his eyes in hell in Luke 16:23 (Hades)
Casting out demons in your name and I never knew you in Matthew 7:22 and 23.
Done evil and will be condemned in John 5:28 and 29.
God's wrath.
Paul uses the term Wrath in his epistles. This is to indicate God's anger about sin or alternatively the consequences of sin or the human response to God
These texts with the word wrath are:
Romans 1:18, 2:5, 2:8, 2:12, 3:5, 4:15, 5:9, 9:22, 13:5.
Ephesians 2:3 and 5:6. Colossians 3:6.
1 Thessalonians 1:10, 2:16, 5:2, 5:9.
Other Pauline texts are:
"Deserve to die" in Romans 1:32
Anguish and distress in Romans 2:9
"Sin apart from the law" in Romans 2:12
"Death" in Romans 6:21-23
"Destruction" Philippians 3:19, 2 Thessalonians 1:9
"Avenger" 1 Thessalonians 4:6 and 5:9.
Other New Testament texts are:
Eternal fire in Jude 7, James 3:6, Hebrews 6:8, Hebrews 12:25-29.
Punishment in Hebrews 2:2.
Shrink back and so are lost in Hebrews 10:27-31
Keys of death and Hell in Revelation 1:18.
Death and Hell in Revelation 6:8 and 20:13.
Lake of fire in Revelation 19:20 and 21:8.
Judgement
Hebrews 6:12
Texts on the Second Coming
Matthew 24: Mark 13:26-27: Luke 17:20: 1 Thessalonians 4:16 and 4:13 to 5:11: 2 Thessalonians 2:1: 2 Peter 3:12

Appendix 2

Some examples of Paintings

Heaven
Anonymous "The heavenly Jerusalem" is displayed in Ghent University Library. 1200
Anonymous "Redeemed couple holding hands" is displayed in the Central portion of Notre Dame Cathedral.
Anonymous "Paradise." Detail of the last Judgement. This picture depicts the blessed beholding their Saviour. It is displayed in Cathedral of Torcello. 1200.
Giotto (Ambrogio di Bondone.) (1267-1337) He made two pictures. "Vision of a heavenly palace". (Cambridge Psalter) and also "Vision of thrones in Heaven." These are part of the painting "The last Judgement".
Nardo and Andrea di Cione Orcagna. (1308-1369) "Glory of Paradise" 1350. It is displayed in the Santa Maria Novella, Italy.
Anonymous "Paradise" is displayed in church of Loreto Aputino. It is part of a detail of Last Judgement. 1420-1430.
Matthias Grunewald. (1470 –1528) "The Resurrection". It is the Isenheim Altarpiece.
Hieronymus Cock. (1510 –1570) "Paradise." 16 Th. century. After Hieronymous Bosch's lost work.
Giovanni du Paolo. (1403-1483)
"Souls and the Trinity". 1438-1444. (Illuminated manuscript).
"Souls in Paradise". (Illuminated manuscript)
"The Blessed Virgin in Paradise". (Illuminated manuscript)
"Paradise". It is displayed in the Metropolitan Museum of Art. 1545.
Lucas Cranach the Elder. (1472-1553)
"The Golden Age 1534."
"The Paradise" 1530. It is displayed in the Alte Pinokothek, Venice. He visualised Paradise as similar to the Garden of Eden, where there was a pastoral scene with deer, dogs, pheasants and geese. Fruit trees and flowering bushes are a notable feature of the picture. Like the Garden of Eden, the couples in the picture were naked, except that one of the women had leaves to protect her modesty. There were four couples in all. In the foreground, one couple was receiving a lecture from an old man who may represent God. In the middle another old man was separating a couple, another couple was hiding close to a bush and the fourth couple were being chased by a winged man. This picture is displayed in the Alte Pinokothek.

Fra Angelico (Giovanni Angelico da Fiesula). (1387-1455)
"In Paradise." 1431. It is displayed in the Museum da San Marco, Florence.
"The dance of the Blessed". 1431. It is displayed in the Alinari, Florence.
"Heaven" (in the last Judgement). It is displayed in the Museum da San Marco, Florence.)
This is a picture of several angels in a circle holding hands.
"Christ glorified in the court of heaven". In this picture, there are a large number of men and women, who are the members of the court of heaven. It is displayed in the National Gallery, London.
Giotto (Ambrogio di Bondone) (1266-1336)
"St. Francis Vision of a Heavenly Palace". Cambridge Psalter.
"Vision of Thrones of Heaven". This is part of the Last Judgement and is displayed in Capella Scrovegni, Padua.
"The plains of Heaven".
Dieric Bouts. (1410-1475) "Paradise." There he described a large number of half clothed people waiting to be taken up into Paradise, which is painted as a gap in the clouds, through which a bright light shines. One soul is already being taken towards the light. It is displayed in the Museum Des Beaux-Arts, Lille.
Luca Signorelli. (1441-1523) "The coronation of the elect". 1499. It is displayed in the Cathedral of Orvieto.
Jean Bellegambe. (1480-1535) "Paradise." 1526-1530. It is displayed in the **Staathliche Museum in Berlin.**
Anonymous The blessed in adoration of the Trinity. 1569. After Maerten van Heemskerck. It is displayed in the Statliche Kaistammlungen Kessel.
Peter Canisius SJ. (1521-1597) A Marian vision of life everlasting.
El Greco (1541-1614) "The hand of Count Orgaz" is displayed in Toledo. An angel takes the soul of the Count upwards on the clouds. The Virgin Mary and John the Baptist are intercessors. Christ and the Saints are on high.
Andrea Pozzo (1642-1706) "The glorification of St. Ignatius" The painting is that of the saint being received into heaven. The picture creates the illusion of heaven and earth through the open vaults of the church.
William Blake. (1757-1827) He painted two pictures:
"The meeting of a family in Heaven". 1808. Engraving.
"The river of the water of life" This depicts persons swimming in a river the motive is from the book of Revelation. It is displayed in the Tate Gallery.

Louis Shiavonetti. Engraved "Reunion of the soul with the body " and "Meeting of a family in heaven". These were pictures by William Blake.
John Martin. (1769-1854) He painted pictures bound in a book. "Rivers of bliss" Book illustration.
"Satan viewing the ascent to heaven." This picture has a very dark Satan viewing the ascent into heaven by angels. He also painted heaven as rivers of bliss. This is a print with mountains, a hill, a castle, a hazy watercourse, peaceful shores, with two angels in the foreground.
"The plains of heaven". A Rivers of bliss book illustration
William Adolphe Bougereau. (1825-1879) "A soul brought to heaven" 1879. This picture shows the dead soul of a woman being carried to heaven by two angels. She appears to be material.
Dante Gabriel Rosetti. (1828-1882) "The blessed Damozel." (Meeting of lovers in Heaven) 1870. It is displayed in the Fogg Art museum, Harvard.
John Bryan Shaw. (1872-1919) He painted a picture "The meeting of lovers in heaven". This is based on the blessed Damozel of Dante Gabriel Rosetti. This picture shows the Virgin Mary seated in the centre of the picture with her handmaidens around her and the meeting of the two lovers at the edge of the picture. It is displayed in Guildhall Library.
Stanley Spencer (1891-1959) As well as the post death resurrection series of paintings, he painted pictures describing heaven particularly "Women going for a walk in heaven" and "John Donne arriving in heaven" (1913)
Francesco Mario Russo. (1946-) "The glory of Heaven". People are bowing towards the light of heaven. Heaven is shown as a patch of white, which indicates the light coming from God. It is displayed in the Araldo da Luca.
Lee G Richards. Family reunion in the other world. 1949. It is displayed in the Idaho Falls temple
Reginald Knowles. "Children in the other world" 1938.
Edward Robert Hughes. (1851-1917)
Danny Hahibohm "Heavens Gate", "Home at last", "In My Father's House", "Eye hath not seen".
Rita Bennett and Sally Moser. (c. 2000) They use the Revelation of St. John the Divine as their guide.
The eight pictures (with commentary) are as follows:
1- Flight across the awesome city.
2- Arrival at the eastern gate. (there is a bright light streaming from inside the gate)

3- The pearly gate with precious stones. (There are twelve gates)
4- Encoded message at the gate
5- Front doors to heaven.
6- Map of the New Jerusalem.
7- Majestic throne of God. (God is not depicted, but light streams form his throne)
8- Redeemer, High priest, King.

The artist used spectacular colours, green, blue, purple and yellow to indicate the scenes. The colours seem overdone, but it is difficult to tell from images on the computer. The picture of light from the city through the gate is exceptionally well done. Light is everywhere and the idea of a long tunnel into the city is novel. Inside there is the river of the water of life (William Blake did the same) and finally there is a picture of the throne of God, which is full of light. This is the only way to indicate God, as you cannot see Him.

Some pictures of Hell

Fra Angelico (Guido di Pietro) (1387-1455) "Last Judgement" detail "Hell" This picture is of a very black Satan with his back turned towards the viewer. Above Satan there are six pictures of human beings, one of those pictures is of persons being boiled in a pot, another picture draws men and women in water. The others are crowded together The purpose of the picture is to indicate the terrors of hell.

Hieronymous Von Acken (Bosch). (1450-1510)
Bosch painted two main works on hell. These are the "Garden of Earthly Delights" in the Prado and the "Hay Wain" (1510). These are triptychs (having three panels) with an outside painting, which is visible when the three panels are shut. The picture on the outside is the earth before the flood, while inside, one painting is of the Garden of Eden, another is the Garden of Earthly Delights, which is supposedly a painting of the earth before the flood. In this painting we see all kinds of wickedness. The picture was described as a satire of the sins and ravings of human beings. The final one of the three pictures denotes hell. This is a really weird picture with all kinds of strange things. Bosch is the type of artist, which today we would call surrealist. His art is a world turned upside down. In the Hay Wain, one panel is a picture of the Garden of Eden; the middle panel is a hay cart, with people trying to climb on and struggling with others also trying to climb on. The third is hell, where a tower is built to denote human punishment.

In the Garden of Earthly Delights, the exterior panel is the creation scene, where the earth is a great globe assuming form at the

direction of the Lord of Heaven. The left wing is the Lord introducing Adam and Eve to paradise. The centre panel is the earth with sins of lust and gluttony. The third panel is hell, a place of gloom and terror. In this panel, the devils in hell torment the damned with their former pleasures. Minstrels are tormented by the instruments, which they used to play. Vain beauties have to admire the reflections in a devil's ass. Sodomists are impaled by demon birds and gluttons are devoured by stomachs on legs. There is a contingent of demons torturing half-size humans. Hell is both very cold and very hot. Even the harp is an instrument of torture. Altogether this is a truly dreadful picture.
Albrecht Durer (1471-1528) Woodcuts of the Four horsemen of the Apocalypse who gallop across sky. They are Death and Hell.
Jacob Isaac Swaneburgh (1571-1639) "Hell" This is a pretty frightening picture, that is crowded with human beings in various places such as a cave and a boat. People are falling in all directions. There are also horrible beasts and a ruined city.
Anonymous depiction of "Hell". It is displayed in the In the Battistero di San Giovani. This is a picture of the devil eating human beings. 13th century.
Michelangelo Buonarotti. (1475-1564)
"Biagio in Hell"   (part of the Last Judgement). c. 1534.
"Last Judgement". 1541. It includes scenes of damned descending into Hell.
Henry Fuseli. (1741-1825) He draws a picture of Satan, calling Beelzebub over a sea of fire and with a figure rising from the depths.
Taddeo Zuccaro (1529-1566) "Hell" He had an image of hell, where people were falling down or being thrown into a pit of fire. This is a fresco painted in the Sistine Chapel Rome.
David Ryder. "Hell". 1991. He is a modern primitive artist who has a work entitled Hell. It is full of faces, with two dots for eyes and an unsmiling mouth, which is turned upside-down the just like a child draws. On examination, I thought these faces were skulls. Added to the large number of faces were two devils, a separate trident and a yellow picture containing a child. Yellow is for childhood. The child apparently represents the present, happiness and spring. The picture seems far-fetched was a good example of modern art.
M C Escher (1898-1972) has a picture entitled "Hell". It has some of the traditional features such as figures of people moving up to heaven and down to hell. The main components include an ear and a peculiar sexual "thing" and a large image, which could represent the body. The total picture is a carefully drawn and is very clever.

But it has its own difficulties of interpretation and has no obvious theme. It appears to be a copy of the middle part of the garden of their earthly delights.
Gustave Dore (1832-18830 He painted images from the Inferno and Paradise Lost.
Auguste Rodin. "The gates of Hell." (sculpture)
Bryce. "Hell". This is a picture of hell with both fire and a mountain. It is a modern painting of the nether sphere. It is a picture of dark mountains over a sea of red lava and a red sunset.
The usual pictures are of Hell. These pictures are Hell as a fire, a lake of fire, a garbage dump, in prison and one picture with a person excluded from God's presence. These are not much different from traditional pictures.

Some pictures of the day of Judgement.
As examples of the last Judgement and art are the following works: There are three anonymous works:
"Painting of the Last Judgement" in Torcello Cathedral.
Sculptures in Church of St. Pierre, Moissac. It is dated about 1100. Sculptures of the last Judgement. This shows Christ surrounded by two angels, the four evangelists holding books and also the twenty-four elders from the book at Revelation.
Painting in Arena Chapel, Padua. The highest part of the painting has the judge at the top. Below Him are the highest apostles, below this is an angelic choir praising God, and there is a big cross at the centre. At the bottom are demons on the one side and saints and the apostles on the other side.
Giotto (Ambrogio di Bondone.) (1266-1336) "Last Judgement" 1306. It is displayed in Capello Sarovegni, Padua.
Pietro di Cerroni (Il Cavallini) (1273-1321) He painted a picture of the "Last Judgement" in detail, showing Christ and three apostles.
Pietro Cavallini (1250-1334) "The Last Judgement". Painted c. 1295. Christ sitting in Judgement seats. It does not really describe the judgement, although it is three dimensional and important artistically. It is displayed in Santa Cecilia in Trastevere, Rome.
Gilbertus Died 1336. "Last Judgement"
Fra Angelico (1387-1455) "Last Judgement". Fresco in San Marco, Florence. It is described in the Chapter on Hell.
Rogier van der Weyden (1400 –1464) "Last Judgement" painted 1444-1448. It is displayed in the hotel Dieu, Beaune, France.
Hieronymous Bosch (1450-1516) "Last Judgement" It is part of a triptych. It is described in the chapter on Hell.

Vrancke Van der Stockt (1424-1495) Panel on "Last Judgement." This is a small part of a triptych called Redemption. Christ is at the top of the painting, the Virgin Mary and St. John the Baptist in the middle and the lower part is in two halves, with the saints and the angels on one half and the condemned on the other half.
Bernardino Zenale. (1464-1526) "The Judgement." 1490. It is displayed in the San Pietro in the Gessole Grifi Chapel in Milan.
Luca Signorelli. (1470-1523) He painted "The last judgement".
Michelangelo Buonarotti (1475-1564) "The Last Judgement", which is painted on the west wall of the Sistine Chapel in Rome. The work was painted between enough for a five have hoof 1534 and 1541.Here, Christ is shown as a stern and highly muscular figure, who is at the very moment of banishing the lost from His presence. Above Christ are angels, with the instruments of the passion. These are the Cross, the column, the crown of thorns, the sponge and the nails. At Christ's side is the Virgin Mary. Around him are the great martyrs, Sebastian with his arrows, Bartholomew with his skin and the knife, which flayed him. Also around Him, are St. Lawrence with his gridiron, Catherine with her wheel and Blaise with his carding comb? It is as though they are reminding the judge to redress their wrongs with a fitting sentence on their torturers. On the left is the line of people ascending from the grave, where risen men and women approach to receive their awards of pain or bliss. On the right, a confused mass of figures in every conceivable condition of fear and horror descend to hell. Below, Minos, the judge of the underworld awaits them, complete with asses ears and the features of Messer Biagio da Cesena, the Pope's chamberlain, and the artist's critic. The angels sound their trump of doom and Charon ferries the lost over the stream, from which there is no return. A cloud of the redeemed float upwards to Paradise. The whole work is centered on the doom of the lost.
Lucas Van Leyden (1494-1533) "The Last Judgement".
Peter Paul Rubens. (1577-1640) "The Last Judgement." 1615-1617.
Louis Shiavonetti. Engraving of the Day of Judgement.1813 after painting by William Blake. Also reunion of the soul with the body.
John Martin (1789-1854) "The great day of His wrath" and the "Last Judgement" His picture of the Last Judgement (which is the Great Assize) is not one of gloom, but has a great contrast between the whiteness of heaven and the blackness of hell. The3 cover of the book Hell and the Victorians shows a part of this picture.
Many of the paintings on the Last Judgement have taken their theme from the passage on the Last Judgement in Revelation 20. If

we were to take this passage literally, then it would happen just like the paintings, which we have listed above
William Blake. "The day of Judgement" 1808.
"Illustrations of the divine comedy". 1824-1827
Hartmann Schedel (1440-1514) The Day of Judgement.

Some pictures of the Second Coming
Stanley Spencer (1891-1959) had several paintings and drawings of the Second Coming. He pictured Jesus among the inhabitants of Britain of his time, particularly before and between the tow world wars. Some of these pictures are as follows: "Sarah Tubb and the heavenly visitors": "Christ preaching at Cookham Regatta": Spencer also painted the Port Glasgow Resurrection series of paintings, where the Port Glasgow people climbed out of their graves and he painted the post grave events -"Waking up" (1945): "Tidying" (1945) (where the resurrected people tidied themselves: "Reunion of families" (1945) and "Rejoicing" (1947). He also painted "The hill of Zion" (1946) and the "Angels of the Apocalypse" (1949).

Appendix 3
List of films with glimpses of heaven or hell
Heaven
1)"**Gladiator**" is a film about a Roman general, Maximus, who was a faithful servant of the emperor Marcus Aurelius. When Commodus succeeded Marcus Aurelius, he was jealous of the general, because of the fidelity of the general to the emperor's father and the love of the emperor's sister for the general. Commodus had Maximus wife and son killed and ordered the execution of Maximus who escaped and became a gladiator. Eventually, Maximus was killed in a contest with the Emperor. Then Maximus returned home to his wife and son in the hereafter. The final pictures showed a white garden (signifying the Holy Spirit) and a narrow gate signifying heaven. At the beginning of the film, Maximus says that what we do in life echoes in eternity. (2000)

2)"**Stir of echoes**" A man is hypnotised at a party making him susceptible to influences from beyond death. The spirit of a girl, who seeks revenge for her murder, haunts him. Her skeleton is found under the man's basement and finally her death is avenged. But is the spirit from heaven or from hell and is the film really about justice in the universe? (1999)

3) "**The sixth sense**" Ghosts with unfinished business". A boy who communicates with spirits, who don't know that they are dead, seeks help of a disheartened child psychologist. Although the end is a happy one, the film is quite unpleasant and does not reveal much about heaven. (1999)

4) "**What dreams may come**" Neurologist Chris and artist Annie had the perfect life until they lost their children in an auto accident: they are just starting to recover when Chris dies and goes to heaven. Annie commits suicide and goes to hell. With help from two friends Chris goes to hell and rescues Annie and they are reunited with their children. The pictures of hell are really awful, but those of heaven are good. (1998)

(5) "**Ghost**" where a murdered man comes back from the dead to right a wrong. His partner murdered him for money and to allow him to court the murdered man's wife. (1990)

(6) "**Field of dreams**" Famous baseball players come back from the dead to play the baseball game again in a playing field made from a field of maize. (1989)

(7) "**Cocoon**" A grandfather goes fishing with his grandson. At the same time some aliens are searching for some cocoons they have left behind. The aliens find the cocoons but put them in a swimming pool to rejuvenate. The local old age pensioners go in the pool and

are rejuvenated, but the cocoons are not rejuvenated so they cannot stand the trip to their planet and have to be put back into the ocean. Instead the grandfather and his friends go on the trip to the other planet, where the old people will receive a new life, which is an analogy to heaven. The grandfather leaves his grandson behind to go to heaven. (1985)

(8) "**Resurrection**" This is a film about a near death experience. (1980)

(9) "**City of Angels**" This is weird film about black angels appearing in Los Angeles.

Hell

1) "**Deconstructing Harry**" This film is all about Harry, a dysfunctional writer with three wives who hate him. In one scene Harry goes to hell and meets Satan, but the film is not mainly about hell.

2) "**Groundhog Day**" A weather forecaster is trapped in a time warp in the small town of Punxsutawney, Pennsylvania on Groundhog day. On that day, there are festivities and a groundhog (a kind of rat) makes a weather forecast. The day is repeated and the events happen again and again. Eventually the weather forecaster changes his attitude and eventually escapes the time warp.

Appendix 4
Books for further reading
R S Anderson. *Theology, death and dying.* Blackwell 1986.
Paul Badham. *Christian beliefs about life after death.* SPCK 1978.
Paul Badham and Linda Badham. *Immortality and extinction.* SPCK 1984.
John Baillie. *And the life everlasting.* Oxford 1934.
Hans urs van Balthasar. *Dare we hope that all men shall be saved?* Ignatius Press 1986.
William Barclay. *The mind of St. Paul.* Fontana1965. (Last chapter)
J. Barr. *The Garden of Eden and the hope of Immortality* SCM 1993.
Richard Bauckham editor *God will be all in all. The eschatology of Jurgen Moltmann.* T and T Clark 1999.
Richard Bauckham and Trevor Hart *Hope against hope.* Darton, Longman and Todd 1999.
Mary K Baxter. *A divine revelation of Hell. Time is running out.* Whittaker House 1993.
G C Berkower. *The return of Christ,* Translated by James Van Oosterom. Eerdmans 1972.
S G F Brandon. T*he judgement of he dead: a historical and comparative study of the idea of a post mortem judgement in the major religions.* Wiedenfield and Nelson 1967. (Only one chapter on Christian belief)
Michael H Brown. *After life: what it's like in heaven and hell and purgatory.* 1997.
Emil Brunner. *Eternal hope.* Lutterworth. 1954.
Harry Buis. *The Doctrine of Eternal Punishment.* Presbyterian and Reformed Publishing Co. Philadelphia. 1957.
Rudolph Bultman. *The presence of eternity. History and Eschatology.* The Gifford lectures 1955. Harper and Brothers, New York. 1975.
Nigel M de S Cameron. *Universalism and the doctrine of Hell.* Papers presented at the fourth Edinburgh conference on Christian Dogmatics 1991. Paternoster Press. 1992.
William Henry Cadham. *The open heaven. The Revelation of God in the Johannine Sayings of Jesus.* Basil Blackwell 1969.
Peter Carnley. *The structure of resurrection belief.* Clarendon 1993.
Norman Cohn. *Cosmos, chaos and the world: the ancient roots of apocalyptic faith.* 1994.
F C Copleston. *Aquinas.* Pelican Books. 1955 (page 156 onwards)
William Crockett. *Four views on Hell.* Zonderman 1992.

Oscar Cullman. *Immortality of the soul or resurrection of the dead. The witness of the New Testament.* Epworth 1958.
Oscar Cullman *Christ and time.* SCM 1962
Brian Daley. *The hope of the early church. A handbook of patristic eschatology.* 1991.
Dante. *The Divine Comedy.* Book 1 Hell Book 2 Purgatory Book 3 Heaven Penguin Books.
Horton Davies. *The communion of saints.* Eerdmans. 1996.
Stephen T Davis. (editor) *Death and the afterlife.* McMillan 1989.
Percy Dearmer. *The legend of Hell: an examination of the idea of everlasting punishment.* Cassell 1929.
Joanne Dewart. *Death and resurrection: message of Fathers of the Church.* Fowler Wright. 1986.
Robert C Doyle. *Eschatology and the shape of Christian belief.* Paternoster. 1999.
Charles S Duthie (Editor). *Resurrection and Immortality. A Selection of the Drew Lectures on immortality.* Samuel Bagster. 1979.
D L Edward. *The last things now.* SCM 1969.
Paul Edwards. *Immortality.* Prometheus Books 1997.
Ajith Fernando. *Crucial questions about Hell.* Kingsway 1991.
P T Forsyth. *This life and the next. The effect of this life of faith on another.* Independent Press.1953.
Edward William Fudge. *The fire that consumes. A Biblical and historical study of the doctrine of final punishment.* Authors Guild Backprint Edition 2001.
T F Glasson. *His appearance and His kingdom.* Epworth1953.
Jim Graham. *Dying to live. The Christian teaching of life after death.* Marshall Morgan and Scott. 1984. Also Hodder and Stoughton 1999.
Romano Guardini. *Eternal life: what you need to know about death, judgement, heaven and hell.* Sophia Books. 1954 reprinted 1998.
Paul Helm. *The last things: death, Judgement, Heaven and Hell.* Banner of Truth 1989.
John Hick. *Death and eternal life.* McMillan 1985.
Dave Hunt. *Whatever happened to Heaven*? Oregon Harvest House Publishers 1988. (Very anti-Catholic to the point of absurdity)
Martin Israel. *Communion of Saints.* The churches fellowship for psychical and fellowship studies. 1980.
Martin Israel. *Coming in glory. Christ's presence in the world today.* Darton.

Edmund Jacob. *Theology of the Old Testament.* Hodder and Stoughton. 1958.
Kenneth. E. Kirk. *Vision of God.* Guernsey Press 1991. (Original 1928)
Hans Kung. *Eternal life. A medical, philosophical and theological problem* SCM 1991.
J N D Kelly *Early Christian Doctrines. T and T Clark 1988.*
Frederick Levison. *The prospect of Heaven: musings of an inquiring believer.* Wild Goose Publications 1997.
C S Lewis. *The humanitarian theory of punishment.* Churchman 73 1959.
Andrew T Lincoln. *Paradise now and not yet.* Cambridge University Press 1981. (The book is incomprehensible with many sentences in untranslated Greek and Hebrew)
David W Lotz. *Heaven and Hell in the Christian tradition.* Religion in life 48 1979.
Colleen McDannell and Bernhard Lang. *Heaven. A history.* Yale University Press 1988.
Alastair E McGrath. *Christian theology: an Introduction.* Blackwell 1988.
Andrew McLelland. *Hell.* Article in life and Work 2002.
John McQuarrie. *Christian hope.* Oxford 1978.
J P Martin. *The last judgement in Protestant theology from Orthodoxy to Ritschl.* Edinburgh 1963. (The problem of relating a Saviour God to Jewish eschatology).
Eric Lionel Mascall. *Grace and glory.* SCM 1975.
James Mew. *Traditional aspects of Hell.* 1901 reprinted 1971. (Only one chapter useful)
C Leslie Mitton. *Present justification and final judgement. A discussion of the parable of the sheep and the goats.* Expository Times 68 1956.
Robert A Morey. *Death and the afterlife.* Bethany house. 1984.
Jurgen Moltmann *Theology of hope.* SCM 1969.
Leon L Morris. *The Biblical Doctrine of Judgement.* Tyndale 1960.
J Alec Motyer. *After Death.* Christian Focus Publications 1965.
Georges Panneton. *Heaven or Hell.* (Translated Ann M C Forster) Newman Press, Maryland 1965.
David Pawson. *The road to Hell. Everlasting torment or annihilation.* Hodder and Stoughton. 1992.
Plato. *The Republic Book 10.* Penguin .1955 edition.
David Powys. *Hell, a hard look at a hard question. The fate of the unrighteous in New Testament thought.* Paternoster. 1997.

Hubert J Richards. *Death and after. What will really happen?* Mowbray. 1986.
John A T Robinson. *Jesus and his coming. The emergence of a doctrine.* SCM 1957.
Geoffrey Rowell. *Hell and the Victorians.* Clarendon 1974.
Gordon Rupp. *Last things first.* SCM 1964.
George Bernard Shaw. *St Joan.* The Bodley Head Collection of plays 1924.
C Ryder Smith. *The Bible doctrine of the hereafter.* Epworth 1958.
F Schleiermacher. *The Christian Faith.* T and T Clark 1928.
J Paterson Smyth. *The Gospel of the hereafter.* Hodder and Stoughton.
William Strawson. *Jesus and the future life.* Epworth 1970.
J. Stevenson. A new Eusebius. SPCK 1968.
A. E. Taylor. *The Christian hope of immortality.* Unicorn Press. 1938.
William Temple. *Nature, Man and God.* McMillan 1934.
Frank J Tipler. *Physics of Immortality.* Anchor Books. 1995
Peter Toon. *Longing for Heaven. The missing element in modern Western spirituality. A Devotional look at life after death.* Hodder and Stoughton.1986.
Stephen H Travis. *I believe in the Second Coming of Jesus.* Hodder and Stoughton 1982.
Simon Tugwell OP. *Human Immortality and the redemption of death.* Darton, Longman and Todd. 1989.
Alice K Turner. *The history of Hell.* (Not much use – nice pictures)
Cornelius P Venema. *The Promise of the future.* Banner of Truth Trust. 2002.
Jeremy L Wells. *Hell: the logic of damnation.* Notre Dame, London. Library of Religious Philosophy 9 1992.
Report of the Commission on Christian Doctrine in the Church of England 1938. With a new introduction by G W H Lampe.

www.ingramcontent.com/pod-product-compliance
Ingram Content Group UK Ltd.
Pitfield, Milton Keynes, MK11 3LW, UK
UKHW041436180426
11947UKWH00007B/480